2 Corinthians

A Digest of Reformed Comment

2 Corinthians

A Digest of Reformed Comment

GEOFFREY B. WILSON

MINISTER OF BIRKBY BAPTIST CHURCH
HUDDERSFIELD

THE BANNER OF TRUTH TRUST

THE BANNER OF TRUTH TRUST
3 Murrayfield Road, Edinburgh EH12 6EL
P.O. Box 621, Carlisle, Pennsylvania 17013, U.S.A.

*

© Geoffrey Backhouse Wilson 1979
First published 1979
ISBN 0 85151 295 X

*

Set in 11 on 12 pt Bembo
and printed in Great Britain by
Hazell Watson & Viney Ltd,
Aylesbury, Bucks

CONTENTS

PREFACE

I am grateful to the authors and publishers who have kindly permitted me to quote from their works, and in particular to the Rev. Professor P. E. Hughes of Westminster Theological Seminary, whose excellent commentary in the New International series is compulsory reading for all serious students of this intensely moving Epistle. I am also indebted to Dr. Williams's Library and to the Evangelical Library for their generous assistance. In this revised edition the American Standard Version (1901), published by Thomas Nelson Inc., has been adopted in the interests of greater accuracy, and chapter summaries have been added.

Huddersfield   GEOFFREY WILSON
February 1979

INTRODUCTION

After staying over eighteen months Paul left the flourishing church he had founded in Corinth for Ephesus (Acts 18.18f.), where, it seems, he received disquieting news of the lax conduct of his Corinthian converts. It was to deal with this grave situation that he sent them a letter (since lost) in which he warned them of the serious consequences of such licentious behaviour [1 Cor 5.9]. Following the despatch of that letter, more bad news reached Paul though some of Chloe's household, who informed him that the church was split into factions [1 Cor 1.11], but this was mercifully offset by the arrival of the Corinthian deputies, Stephanas, Fortunatus, and Achaicus [1 Cor 16.17]. For though the letter they presumably brought with them made no reference to these grievous divisions within the fellowship, the fact that the church had taken the trouble to seek his advice on certain points of conduct and worship showed that it still acknowledged his authority [1 Cor 7.1].

By way of reply Paul wrote the Epistle we know as First Corinthians, in which he states that he has already sent Timothy to them as his special envoy [1 Cor 4.17; 16.10]. But when Timothy arrived he was faced with an entirely new situation, for he found that Paul's authority in the church had been undermined by the superior claims put forward by a group of Jewish opponents to the Pauline mission. In view of this fresh crisis Timothy could do nothing but return with the news to Ephesus. On hearing Timothy's report Paul resolved to pay an immediate visit to Corinth, but it appears that this attempt to settle the issue in person met with a humiliating rebuff. The sequel to this 'painful' visit [2 Cor 2.1] was a 'severe' letter of reproof which is also lost to us (it was probably destroyed after it had achieved its object). Although it cost Paul 'much affliction and anguish of heart' to write such a letter [2 Cor 2.4], he knew it had to be done if the rebellious Corinthians were to be restored to apostolic obedience. Paul entrusted the letter to Titus, but as he anxiously waited to hear how the Corinthians had received it, he was assailed by doubts and beset with danger [2 Cor 1.8-10].

After the riot in Ephesus brought his work there to an abrupt end [Acts 20.1], Paul hastened to Troas where he had arranged to meet Titus on his return from Corinth [2 Cor 2.12, 13]. The disappointment of this hope led him to travel on to Macedonia, where at last they met, probably in Philippi, or its port, Neapolis. The report that Titus gave to Paul on the Corinthians' response to his letter was largely reassuring. Although the false teachers, who had infiltrated into the church by arming themselves with letters of commendation [2 Cor 3.1], were encouraging a minority to remain recalcitrant [2 Cor 12.21], the majority were humbled by the severe letter and had been 'made sorry unto repentance' [2 Cor 7.9].

Under the inspiration of the Spirit, Paul here gives free expression to the mingled emotions which were aroused in him by this report. It is this deliberate lack of reserve that makes the document we call Second Corinthians the most intensely personal of all Paul's utterances. It is at once a triumphant vindication of his apostolic ministry, and a searing indictment of the pretensions of the 'super-apostles' who were attempting to overthrow his work in Corinth by basely slandering his character and his motives. Thus the purpose of the letter was to prepare the Corinthians for his promised visit.

It was written to ensure that when he came to Corinth for the *third* time it would be in joy and not in sorrow or anger [2 *Cor* 2.1; 12.14; 13.1, 2].

If the above is an accurate outline of Paul's relations with the Corinthian church, we have the following sequence of events:—

    Paul's first visit [*Acts* 18.1ff]
    The previous letter [1 *Cor* 5.9]
    1 Corinthians   *c.* Spring AD 55
    The painful visit [2 *Cor* 2.1]
    The severe letter [2 *Cor* 2.4]
    Paul leaves Ephesus and meets
      Titus in Macedonia [*Acts* 20.1]
    2 Corinthians   *c.* Autumn AD 56
    Paul's third visit [*Acts* 20.2]

As 'Second' Corinthians is manifestly an intelligible unity, there is no need to accept the modern notion that 2 *Cor* 6.14–7.1 is a fragment of the 'previous' letter [1 *Cor* 5.9] and that part of the 'severe' letter is preserved in 2 *Cor* 10.1–13.10, especially as there is no external evidence to show that it was ever circulated in any other form.

CHAPTER ONE

After affirming his divine calling as an apostle of Christ, Paul associates Timothy with himself in greeting the church at Corinth and all the saints of Achaia [vv 1, 2]. Paul blesses God for the comfort received throughout his recent afflictions, by which he is enabled to comfort the Corinthians in their distress [vv 3–7]. He refers to his deliverance from a peril in Asia that made him despair of life, and expresses his confidence in God's future protection through their prayers [vv 8–11]. Apparently the apostle's detractors charged him with inconsistency on the grounds that he had changed his travel plans, but he insists that the real reason for postponing his visit was to spare them [vv 12–24].

V1: Paul, an apostle of Christ Jesus through the will of God, and Timothy our brother, unto the church of God which is at Corinth, with all the saints that are in the whole of Achaia:

Paul, an apostle of Christ Jesus through the will of God,
Since the Corinthians had questioned his authority so recently, it is not surprising that Paul should begin with the reminder that he is not an apostle of Christ Jesus by human accreditation but by divine appointment [cf 3.1]. It is through the eternal good pleasure of God that he is such an apostle. Moreover, because he was *directly* called by the risen Christ himself, his apostleship differed radically from that which was exercised by

those who were *mediately* commissioned by the church [8.23; *Phil* 2.25]. And though he counts it a privilege to serve the church [4.5], it is significant that he never speaks of himself as 'an apostle of the church'. All the evidence 'points overwhelmingly to the fact that, *in the highest sense of the word*, only the original apostles and Paul were called and appointed to be the "authorized representatives" of the exalted Lord. Where Barnabas is called an apostle in *Acts* 14.4, 14 it is clearly in the sense of one being sent by the Church as a fully commissioned missionary but not as an "apostle of Christ" [cf *Acts* 13.14] in the highest sense as used of the Twelve and Paul' (Norval Geldenhuys, *Supreme Authority*, pp. 71–72). Thus as it was the unique function of the apostles to be *eye*-witnesses of the resurrection and by their inspired testimony to provide the foundation upon which the church rests, it is evident that they can have no successors in this office.

and Timothy the brother, (ASV margin) It is not to share the responsibility of composition that Paul includes Timothy in the address, but to enhance his appeal to the Corinthians. What he writes with all the authority of an apostle also commands the fraternal assent of a fellow-Christian who is also well known to them [1 *Cor* 1.1]. The linking of Timothy's name with his own is also a tacit rebuke, for it expresses his continued confidence in an envoy they had treated badly (see Introduction), but who nevertheless still had their spiritual welfare at heart.

unto the church of God which is at Corinth, In writing to this company of believers living in a particular place, Paul reminds them of the dignity that is theirs as *the* church of God, and of their obligations as members of the church *of God*. According to K. L. Schmidt, the designation affords strong support for 'the contention that the Church is not a great community made up of an accumulation of small communities, but is truly present in its wholeness in every company of believers, however small' (cited by P. E. Hughes).

with all the saints that are in the whole of Achaia: Paul addresses the Corinthian church *directly*, and all the Christians in the province *indirectly*. This indicates that he 'was conscious that his written words were significant for the whole Church of God, and not merely for the particular local churches at which they were first delivered' (R. V. G. Tasker). In the New Testament, sainthood is not the prerogative of a special caste but the privilege of every Christian [cf. *Acts* 9.13]. As each believer is objectively 'holy' in Christ, so he is to be subjectively transformed 'into the same image' [3.18]. But because believers have not yet attained this goal [*Phil* 3.12], they are not sinlessly perfect, and must continue to trust in the mediation of their righteous Advocate with the Father [1 *John* 1.8–2.1].

*V*2: **Grace to you and peace from God our Father and the Lord Jesus Christ.**

Grace to you and peace. It is by replacing the ordinary 'hail' of Greek letter-writing with the word 'grace' that Paul invests the customary greeting with a deep religious meaning. 'Grace' is the free and unmerited favour of God, and the blessed result of its reception is 'peace'.

from God our Father and the Lord Jesus Christ. The pronoun 'our' advertises the stupendous fact that God the Father is also the Father of believers in virtue of his adoptive grace towards them in the Lord Jesus Christ. The blessings of grace and peace descend to us from God our Father 'as the primal *Fountain*', through Christ 'as the mediatorial *Channel*'; and 'by coupling both Persons in one and the same invocation, their equality in the Godhead is brightly confirmed' (David Brown).

*V*3: **Blessed** *be* **the God and Father of our Lord Jesus Christ, the Father of mercies and God of all comfort;**

Blessed *be* **the God and Father of our Lord Jesus Christ,** Paul usually follows his greeting with a thanksgiving for what God has done for his readers, but here he bursts into a jubilant doxology to praise God for the marvellous mercies so recently vouchsafed to himself [*v* 4]. As in *Eph* 1.3 and 1 *Pet* 1.3, the customary Jewish blessing, 'Blessed be God', is given a distinctively Christian content. This remarkable expression indicates that God is both the God and Father of the Lord Jesus Christ. He became his God when the Son was made flesh for our salvation, whereas he is his Father from all eternity. But we cannot call upon God as *our* Father [*v* 2], except as we are related to him through the merits and mediation of *our* Lord Jesus Christ [*John* 14.6].

the Father of mercies. Instead of speaking, as we should, of 'the mercy of God' as an abstract principle, 'Paul speaks of its various concrete manifestations. These reveal the essential nature of the great Father and are therefore taken up into his Name' (J. A. Beet). [*Ps* 103.13]

and God of all comfort; The word 'comfort' which Paul uses ten times in five verses is not to be understood in any sentimental sense. God comforts his people by encouraging and strengthening them, so that they are not crushed by affliction. Arthur Pink points out that this is an excellency peculiar to the true and living God, for the heathen deities are represented as being so cruel and ferocious that even their own worshippers regard them as objects of dread. Yet 'many believers seem to be as reluctant to go out of themselves to God alone for comfort, as unbelievers are to go out of themselves to Christ alone for righteousness' (*Gleanings from Paul*, p. 68).

V4: **who comforteth us in all our affliction, that we may be able to comfort them that are in any affliction, through the comfort wherewith we ourselves are comforted of God.**

'Affliction' is the distress produced by painful pressure, and this is relieved by the 'comfort' which prevents it from becoming insupportable. Knowing the sustaining strength of God in *all* his affliction qualified the apostle to be of comfort to others in *every kind* of affliction. He did not see this comfort as a blessing to be selfishly kept to himself, but as the divinely given means of helping those in similar straits. Paul would have the Corinthians know that he finds such comforting more congenial than administering the faithful wounds of a friend [*Prov* 27.6]. For though he had not flinched from this duty, he did not rejoice in it.

V5: **For as the sufferings of Christ abound unto us, even so our comfort also aboundeth through Christ.**

For just as the sufferings of Christ flow over into our lives, so also through Christ our comfort overflows. (NIV) There is no thought of sharing in Christ's atoning sacrifice, for the gospel Paul preached was plainly based on the finished work of Christ [*Rom* 5.8–10; 6.10]. But though the personal sufferings of Christ are past, his sufferings in his people still continue. The unforgettable lesson which Paul learned on the Damascus road was that the glorified Christ reckoned as his own whatever sufferings his people endured for his sake [*Acts* 9.4, 5]. These tribulations are the lot of the Messianic community on earth [*Acts* 14.22], because those who confess their interest in the Messiah cannot avoid their share of the same hatred that reached its climax in his crucifixion [*Heb* 13.13]. Yet the willing bearers of Christ's reproach always find that their suffering is matched by his comfort. 'As union with Christ was the source of the afflictions which Paul endured, so it was the source of the abundant consolation which he enjoyed. This makes the great difference between the sorrows of believers and those of unbelievers. Alienation from Christ does not secure freedom from suffering, but it cuts us off from the only source of consolation. Therefore the sorrow of the world worketh death' (Charles Hodge).

*V*6: **But whether we are afflicted, it is for your comfort and salvation; or whether we are comforted, it is for your comfort, which worketh in the patient enduring of the same sufferings which we also suffer: 7 and our hope for you is steadfast; knowing that, as ye are partakers of the sufferings, so also are ye of the comfort.**

The bond which unites Paul with the Corinthians is so vital that whatever befalls him in the service of Christ is experienced with a view to their good. He endures affliction for their encouragement and salvation; he receives comfort for their strengthening, the effectiveness of which is shown in their patient endurance of the same suffering for the sake of the gospel as he himself endures. In verse 7 Paul sums up the paragraph on a note of triumphant hope. It is because the Corinthians are sharers with him both in his sufferings and in his comfort that he has no doubt of their final salvation. They will be enabled to endure to the end, for the comfort is always commensurate with the suffering. 'He does not claim the credit of comforting them: they receive comfort from the same source that he does – from God through Christ' (Alfred Plummer).

*V*8: **For we would not have you ignorant, brethen, concerning our affliction which befell *us* in Asia, that we**

were weighed down exceedingly, beyond our power, insomuch that we despaired even of life:

Having spoken in a general way of affliction and comfort, Paul now vividly recalls a recent affliction by which he was so excessively weighed down that he even despaired of life. Clearly he had been in mortal peril of some kind, though in the absence of further information it is impossible to identify the nature of this terrible experience. But in the light of Ch. 11.23–26, which reveals something of what the apostle suffered to bring the gospel to the Gentiles [*Acts* 9.16], we can see that he did not exaggerate when he used such expressions as 'death worketh in us' [4.12] and 'I die daily' [1 *Cor* 15.31]. However, what follows shows that Paul's concern was not to provide a circumstantial account of the danger, but to magnify God's grace in his deliverance from it [*v* 9].

*V*9: **yea, we ourselves have had the sentence of death within ourselves, that we should not trust in ourselves, but in God who raiseth the dead:**

James Denney draws attention to the force of the perfect tense: 'We *had* this experience, and in its fruit – a newer and deeper faith in God – we *have* it still. It is a permanent possession in this happy form'. If Paul now recalls the sentence he had passed on himself in his despair it is only that the Corinthians might learn the blessed lesson he was taught by it. For no trial, however severe, can frustrate the sovereign purpose of God who does in fact work all things together for the good of his people [*Rom* 8.28].

that we should not trust in ourselves, but in God who raiseth the dead: Thus the affliction that dealt the fatal stroke to all self-trust was sent to inspire undying hope in the God by whose omnipotent power alone the dead are raised to life. It is this capacity to create life where previously death reigned supreme that distinguishes the one true and living God from all the helpless deities of man's invention [*Ps* 135.15–18; *Ezek* 37.1–14; *Rom* 4.17; *Heb* 11.19].

*V*10: **who delivered us out of so great a death, and will deliver: on whom we have set our hope that he will also still deliver us;**

Having experienced so great a deliverance, Paul cannot doubt that the God upon whom he has set his hope will continue to deliver him from whatever perils still lie ahead, until he is finally delivered from suffering and brought to glory [2 *Tim* 4.18]. 'Past experiences are great encouragements to faith and hope, and they lay great obligations to trust in God for time to come. We reproach our experiences, if we distrust God in future straits, who hath delivered us in former troubles' (Matthew Henry).

*V*11: **ye also helping together on our behalf by your supplication; that, for the gift bestowed upon us by means of many, thanks may be given by many persons on our behalf.**

Paul here gently reminds the Corinthians that they are not idle spectators of a drama in which they have no part to play. For it is by their joining together in prayer on his behalf that he expects to obtain this deliverance which remains the gracious gift of God, even though its bestowal involves the supplication of many. Yet the great end for which such answers to prayer are given is never secured by the mere reception of the blessing itself, but in that grateful response which magnifies the glory of the Blesser himself. Hence the undeserved favours that descend to us from God must ever ascend to God as a heartfelt paean of praise [cf 4.15; 9.11].

*V*12: **For our glorying is this, the testimony of our conscience, that in holiness and sincerity of God, not in**

**fleshly wisdom but in the grace of God, we behaved
ourselves in the world, and more abundantly to you-
ward.**

Paul can enlist the support of the Corinthians in prayer with
confidence. He is satisfied that his conduct both in the world
and in their midst is sufficient reply to those who assailed his
integrity and impugned his sincerity in order to establish
themselves as the new leaders of the church.

For our glorying is this, Since Paul is not ashamed of what
the grace of God has wrought in his life, he does not hesitate
to counter the empty boasting of his opponents in Corinth
with a true glorying in the Lord (contrast 11.18 with 10.17).
And this probably accounts for his frequent use of the word
'glorying' or 'boasting' in this Epistle, the various forms of the
word appearing some thirty times in it.

the testimony of our conscience, This testimony is true,
for he knows the real peace of a conscience pacified by the
blood of Christ, and the sure guidance of a conscience en-
lightened by the Word of God.

**that in holiness and sincerity of God, not in fleshly wis-
dom but in the grace of God, we behaved ourselves in
the world,** Paul thus freely attributes the 'moral purity'
(Arndt-Gingrich) of his conduct and the sincerity of his
motives to the grace of God. He has moved in the sphere of
this grace ever since the day he renounced all confidence in
the flesh, including that fleshly wisdom upon which the Corinthians set such store, and which he had tried so hard to dis-
courage in them [1 *Cor* 2.1ff].

and more abundantly to you-ward. He was of course
equally sincere elsewhere, but the Corinthians had been given

[23]

a better opportunity than most to observe his sincerity. 'He has deliberately put it in this way to show that there was no need for witnesses from a distance, for they themselves were the best witnesses to all that he had said' (John Calvin).

*V*13: **For we write no other things unto you, than what ye read or even acknowledge, and I hope ye will acknowledge unto the end: 14 as also ye did acknowledge us in part, that we are your glorying, even as ye also are ours, in the day of our Lord Jesus.**

For we write you nothing but what you can read and understand; (RSV) Moreover, Paul insists that he is as sincere in his letters as he is in his life. He is not the shifty correspondent his detractors claim him to be, writing one thing and meaning another. He always writes what he means, and means exactly what he writes. 'You don't have to read between the lines of my letters; you can understand them' (Moffatt). But their reception of his letters has shown that they were not always willing to understand the plain meaning of what he had written. The obscurity of Scripture lies not in the supposed difficulty of its message, but in that spiritual insensitivity which cherishes the sins Scripture so clearly condemns.

I hope you will understand fully, as you have understood in part, that you can be proud of us as we can be of you, on the day of the Lord Jesus. (RSV) Paul here contrasts 'the imperfect estimate of his sincerity which the Corinthians now have with that which will be theirs when the secrets of all hearts are revealed at the Last Day' (Chrysostom). When they at last realize all that they owe to his ministry, they will be as proud of him as he is of them [1 *Thess* 2.19, 20].

[24]

*V*15: **And in this confidence I was minded to come first unto you, that ye might have a second benefit; 16: and by you to pass into Macedonia, and again from Macedonia to come unto you, and of you to be set forward on my journey unto Judaea.**

It was on the ground of this mutual confidence that Paul had hoped to pay the Corinthians a double visit, on his way to and from Macedonia, so that they might receive a 'second benefit' and be given the privilege of sending him forward on his journey to Judaea. But as this proposal differs from his original intention of visiting Corinth on his way from Macedonia [1 *Cor* 16.5], it would seem that Paul made this change in his travel plans *after* the despatch of 1 Corinthians. The fact that he had now changed his mind again and reverted to the original plan was seized upon by his critics as the proof that he was not a man of his word. Paul answers this charge before showing that the Corinthians themselves were to blame for his apparent vacillation [1.23–2.4].

*V*17: **When I therefore was thus minded, did I show fickleness? or the things that I purpose, do I purpose according to the flesh, that with me there should be the yea yea and the nay nay?**

Was such a change of plan evidence of the fickleness of character attributed to Paul by his opponents in Corinth? Or can the Corinthians believe that their apostle makes his plans in such an unprincipled manner that he has no compunction in affirming one thing at one time and shortly changing to the very opposite? The unjust allegations of his adversaries are not merely echoed but emphatically answered in these indignant questions.

*V*18: **But as God is faithful, our word toward you is not yea and nay.**

The Corinthians should realize that they could not call in question the trustworthiness of their apostle without also reflecting upon the faithfulness of God who had entrusted him with the gospel. For was it not the height of incongruity to imagine that a faithful God had saved them through the ministrations of a faithless servant? Experience should have taught them above all others that he is not a man of Jesuitical reserve who means 'No' when he says 'Yes'. Thus 'God is faithful in the fact that he sends men to preach whose preaching is not double-tongued, a promise and no performance' (J. Massie).

*V*19: **For the Son of God, Jesus Christ, who was preached among you by us,** *even* **by me and Silvanus and Timothy, was not yea and nay, but in him is yea.**

For the Son of God, Jesus Christ, 'Proof of the unchangeableness of the doctrine from the unchangeableness of the subject of it – viz., Jesus Christ. He is called "the Son of God", to show the impossibility of change in One co-equal with God himself [cf 1 *Sam* 15.29; *Mal* 3.6]' (A. R. Fausset).

who was preached among you by us, *even* **by me and Silvanus and Timothy, was not yea and nay,** Paul reminds the Corinthians that they had trusted him and his fellow evangelists, Silvanus (= Silas of *Acts* 18.5) and Timothy, both in their message and their character, for the two went together. 'No mighty yea-Christ could have been transmitted by yea-and-nay heralds' (R. C. H. Lenski).

but in him is yea. The force of the perfect tense is well conveyed by P. E. Hughes: 'In Him yes was and continues to be a reality'. The Corinthians had experienced the eternal 'Yes' of God's saving purpose in Christ through the faithful proclamation of this divine affirmative, and so they could not

doubt the fidelity of God's messengers without also question-
ing the reality of their own faith.

V20: **For how many soever be the promises of God, in
him is the yea: wherefore also through him is the Amen,
unto the glory of God through us.**

Christ is the fulfiller and fulfilment of all the promises of God
because he is the sum and substance of them. From Genesis
to Malachi – from the *protevangelium*, the first promise of a
Redeemer, to prophecy's last witness to his coming – each
and every promise finds its affirmation and accomplishment
in him [*Luke* 24.44; *Gal* 3.16; *Heb* 10.7].

**wherefore also through him is the Amen, unto the glory
of God** Christ's 'Yea' to all the divine promises is appro-
priated by the 'Amen' of faith. In affixing this seal to God's
faithfulness, faith gives glory to God [*John* 3.33; *Rom* 4.20].
It is both through Christ and through those who preach him
('through us') that men are brought to say the 'Amen' of faith.
For though Christ is the great awakener of faith, 'his appeal
reaches the world through his representatives' (H. L. Goudge).
[*Rom* 10.17]

through us. 'This connects the thought with the main argument. Is it likely that we should be unfaithful to promises who
cause glory to be ascribed to God for his faithfulness?' (Massie).

V21: **Now he that establisheth us with you in Christ,
and anointed us, is God; 22 who also sealed us, and gave
us the earnest of the Spirit in our hearts.**

Now he that establisheth us with you in Christ, As the
Corinthians were divinely constrained to *confirm* Paul's preaching of the gospel with the 'Amen' of faith, so it is no less a
work of grace that they with him are being daily *confirmed* in

their union with Christ. Nor could they consider the reality of this shared experience without recognizing that he is sincere and consistent in all his relations with them. Moreover, Paul goes on to show that God's *present* work of establishing all believers in Christ is based entirely upon what he has *already* done for them in conversion. For it was then that he anointed, sealed, and gave the earnest of the Spirit to them.

and anointed us, is God; It is in the anointing of his people with the Holy Spirit that God consecrates them to his service and makes them like Christ, the Anointed One *par excellence* [*Luke* 4.18, 19; 1 *John* 2.20, 27]. Hence this blessing is bestowed through Christ, 'on whom the oil of gladness, and all the graces of the Spirit are first poured out, and then from him are carried to the meanest member of his body' (David Dickson on *Psalm* 133). [cf *John* 7.39]

who also sealed us, The sealing of the Spirit is the act by which God marks out a people for himself and secures them unto the day of redemption. The Holy Spirit 'marks those in whom he dwells as belonging to God. They bear the seal of God upon them. *Rev* 7.2, 2 *Tim* 2.19 ... He also bears witness in the hearts of believers that they are the children of God. He authenticates them to themselves and others as genuine believers. And he effectively secures them from apostasy and perdition. *Eph* 1.13, 4.30' (Hodge).

and gave *us* the earnest of the Spirit in our hearts. The 'deposit' or 'pledge' of the Spirit is at once the foretaste and guarantee of the Christian's interest in the heavenly inheritance [cf 5.5; *Rom* 8.23; *Eph* 1.14]. 'The actual spiritual life of the Christian is the same in kind as his future glorified life; the kingdom of heaven is a present kingdom; the believer is already seated on the right hand of God ... Nevertheless the present gift of the Spirit is only a *small fraction* of the future endowment. This idea also would be suggested by the usual

relation between the earnest-money and the full payment'
(J. B. Lightfoot).

*V*23: **But I call God for a witness upon my soul, that to
spare you I forbare to come unto Corinth.**

Having demonstrated the impossibility of any duplicity on
his part, the apostle now reveals the real reason for postponing
his visit. Since no one else knew what caused him to change
his mind, he strongly affirms the truthfulness of his testimony
by invoking the punishment of God against himself if what
he says is false. In fact it was solely to spare them that Paul
stayed away from Corinth in the hope that this delay would
give them the opportunity to repent, for he had determined
that he would not pay them another painful visit (see further
comment on 2.1).

*V*24: **Not that we have lordship over your faith, but are
helpers of your joy: for in faith ye stand fast.**

To guard against any misunderstanding of the word 'spare'
[*v* 23], Paul assures the Corinthians that he has neither the
power nor the desire to exercise any lordship over their faith
(though he knows that the 'false apostles' set no such limits
to *their* authority – 11.20). But he seeks only to remove those
sinful disorders which hinder their true rejoicing. If therefore
the pattern of ministry set by the authentic apostles was not
that of lording it over the flock [1 *Pet* 5.3], then how can this
power lawfully be claimed and exercised by their pretended
successors?

for in faith ye stand fast. 'Well may we disclaim any such
undue interference; for ye stand, not on us, but each to his
own Master on the footing of his own faith; nor can any one,
not even an apostle of Jesus Christ, come in between him and
God, the Judge of all' (David Brown). [*Rom* 14.4].

CHAPTER TWO

Paul now explains why he put off the expected visit. He had determined that he would not come again to the Corinthians with sorrow. And as he could not cause them pain without being grieved himself, he thought it better to write a painful letter than to have another sorrowful meeting with those who ought to give him joy [vv 1–4]. The apostle is satisfied with the censure inflicted by the majority on the man who caused particular offence, and he urges them to forgive and comfort him, just as he has forgiven him in the presence of Christ lest any advantage should be gained by Satan [vv 5–11]. Paul was so anxious to hear how Titus had fared in Corinth that when he failed to find him in Troas, he could not continue preaching there, but went off to seek him in Macedonia [vv 12, 13]. Paul's intense joy on learning that Titus was, after all, the bearer of good news leads him to bless God, who always causes his sincere servant to triumph in Christ [vv 14–17].

*V*1: **But I determined this for myself, that I would not come again to you with sorrow.**

From this it is clear that Paul had already made one painful visit to Corinth, and since no reference to such a visit is implied in 1 Corinthians, it presumably took place after that letter was despatched [12.14; 13.1f]. Although Paul had no desire to repeat this unhappy experience, he had deferred his visit in the Corinthians' interest, and not simply to escape further personal suffering. His decision was made in the hope that this delay would give them the opportunity to put matters right themselves, following their reception of his 'severe' letter (see comment on *vv* 3, 4).

*V*2: **For if I make you sorry, who then is he that maketh me glad but he that is made sorry by me?**

Paul here assures the Corinthians that his own joy is bound up with their spiritual prosperity. 'As the helper of their joy he would receive joy through their faith and obedience. So long as their moral condition compelled him to come, bringing rebuke and pain, they could not be a source of joy to him. If I must needs make you sorry with merited rebuke, who can give me joy save you who are thus made sorry?' (Marvin R. Vincent). Hence the restoration of his joy depended upon their repentance and amendment.

*V*3: **And I wrote this very thing, lest, when I came, I should have sorrow from them of whom I ought to rejoice; having confidence in you all, that my joy is *the joy* of you all.**

And I wrote as I did, so that when I came I might not be pained by those who should have made me rejoice, (RSV) As the Corinthians' faithful apostle, Paul knew that there was no painless way of dealing with the problem of sin [7.8ff]. But he wrote them a painful letter to avoid another painful visit, for he hoped that its effect would be such that when he next came to Corinth they would meet in joy, not in sorrow.

for I felt sure of all of you, that my joy would be the joy of you all. (RSV) (Cf the 'all' of 13.14) 'Even at this time

[31]

of revolt he had confidence that they had no real joy apart from his, and would therefore put away what was grievous to him' (Massie).

*V*4: **For out of much affliction and anguish of heart I wrote unto you with many tears; not that ye should be made sorry, but that ye might know the love which I have more abundantly unto you.**

This is a touching disclosure of what it cost the apostle to write his 'severe' letter. It is impossible to accept the traditional identification of this letter with 1 Corinthians for two reasons:—

1. The discursive style and generally calm tone of 1 Corinthians does not suggest that it was written under the stress of great emotion, as 2 Corinthians undoubtedly was. And this change reflects the crisis which had arisen in the intervening period.

2. It is clear from 2 Corinthians that the 'severe' letter was the sequel to the 'painful' visit. So if the 'severe' letter is taken to be 1 Corinthians, the 'painful' visit must have *preceded* it. But as there is not the slightest hint of such a second visit in 1 Corinthians, it must have taken place *after* its despatch. Hence the 'severe' letter which followed that visit cannot be identified with 1 Corinthians.

not that ye should be made sorry, but that ye might know the love which I have more abundantly unto you. It gave Paul no satisfaction to make them sorry, but he loved them too much to let them lie down in their sins. Consequently they would not understand his motive in writing the 'severe' letter, unless they saw even this as the fruit of his love for them [cf *Heb* 12.11]. 'More abundantly' should not of course be taken to mean that Paul loved the Corinthians more than his converts in other places. It rather refers to the greater demands which they made upon his love by their folly.

V5: **But if any hath caused sorrow, he hath caused sorrow, not to me, but in part (that I press not too heavily) to you all.**

Although the deliberately vague language of this verse makes it difficult for us to identify the culprit, he cannot be equated with the incestuous man of 1 *Cor* 5.1ff, because it appears that his offence was directed against the apostle himself [cf *v* 10]. Evidently Paul refers to the incident which made his second visit to Corinth such a sorrowful one, and we may reasonably suppose that this man took the lead in challenging his authority before the whole church. At the time the Corinthians had failed to stand by Paul, not realizing that an attack on their apostle was also an attack on the church he had founded [cf 1 *Cor* 3.10, 11]. Hence Paul says that the offender has caused sorrow, 'not to me', meaning 'not *only* to me', 'but in some degree (in order not to say too much) to you all' (Arndt-Gingrich).

V6: **Sufficient to such a one is this punishment which was *inflicted* by the many; 7 so that contrariwise ye should rather forgive him and comfort him, lest by any means such a one should be swallowed up with his overmuch sorrow.**

Awakened to its responsibility by Paul's 'severe' letter and the ministry of Titus, the church had acted to clear itself and punish the rebel [7.11]. In saying that this church censure was imposed by the 'majority' [RSV], Paul does not imply that the minority were disloyal to him. His language in verse 7 rather suggests that they were 'supporters' [1 *Cor* 1.12, 13] who thought that the punishment was far too lenient! He

2C.—3

checks this excessive zeal by showing that the offender's repentance demands their forgiveness. Otherwise there is a grave danger that he might be overwhelmed with too much sorrow. The emphatic placing of 'such a one' at the very end of the sentence gives expression to Paul's compassionate concern for the man. 'The character which Paul here exhibits reflects the image of our heavenly Father. His word is filled with denunciations against impenitent sinners, and at the same time with assurances of unbounded pity and tenderness towards the penitent. He never breaks the bruised reed or quenches the smoking flax' (Hodge).

*V*8: **Wherefore I beseech you to confirm** *your* **love toward him.**

... *your* **love.** The vital word is again the last word in the sentence. Instead of agreeing with the rigorists of Corinth, Paul pleads not merely for the formal reinstatement of the offender, but that the congregation should leave him in no doubt of the warmth of their love. For by thus 'loosing' his sin, the church would assure or confirm to him the reality of God's forgiveness [*John* 20.23].

*V*9: **For to this end also did I write, that I might know the proof of you, whether ye are obedient in all things.**

Paul's purpose in writing the 'severe' letter was to test whether the Corinthians were obedient in all things. And now that they had proved their genuineness by punishing the offender, he is confident that the joyful duty of forgiving this man will command their willing response. Paul does not actually say that they are obedient to him, because he is an apostle whose sole desire is to promote in them the 'obedience of faith' [*Rom* 1.5; cf 10.5].

*V*10: **But to whom ye forgive anything, I** *forgive* **also: for what I also have forgiven, if I have forgiven any-**

thing, for your sakes *have I forgiven it* in the presence of Christ;

The greatness of Paul's character is seen in his ready forgiveness of the rebel and his generous dismissal of the very real injury he himself had suffered. Grace demands that we both forgive and forget, because breaches of fellowship cannot be healed unless even the memory of the offence is blotted out. What a difference it would make if only all believers realized that nursed grievances are nothing less than a canker in the body of Christ!

As there was a danger that the Corinthians might refuse to forgive the man in their belated zeal to defend their apostle [7.11], Paul removes this excuse by assuring them that he had their spiritual welfare at heart [*v* 11] when he forgave the wrong in the presence of Christ. And this telling reference to the witness of Christ serves to remind them that their own forgiveness must be equally sincere. 'No man can be severe in his judgment who feels that the mild eyes of Christ are fixed upon him' (Hodge).

***V*11: that no advantage may be gained over us by Satan: for we are not ignorant of his devices.**

As the sower of discord among brethren, only Satan stood to gain by a failure to forgive the now repentant wrongdoer. This would give Satan more than his due by allowing him to use the Christian grace of repentance to embitter the church and to drive the man to despair. 'Ignorant' and 'devices' are akin in sound and root; 'we are not without *knowledge* of his *knowing* schemes' (Fausset). [*Eph* 6.11].

***V*12: Now when I came to Troas for the gospel of Christ, and when a door was opened unto me in the Lord, 13 I had no relief for my spirit, because I found**

not Titus my brother: but taking my leave of them, I went forth into Macedonia.

Paul now resumes the account of his movements [1.8]. On leaving Ephesus he travelled to Troas where he not only intended to preach the gospel, but also found a favourable opportunity for doing so as he awaited the return of Titus from Corinth [cf *Acts* 14.27; 1 *Cor* 16.9; *Col* 4.3]. As P. E. Hughes observes, the expression 'in the Lord' is an evidence of the thoroughly Christ-centred nature of Paul's thought: 'The Lord Christ is both the content of the Apostle's message and also the sphere of his opportunity'.

But when Titus failed to arrive Paul became so anxious about the outcome of the crisis in Corinth that he was unable to continue his work among the people of Troas, and bidding them farewell he crossed over to Macedonia. It was therefore 'a great proof of his very special affection for the Corinthians that his concern for them would not let him rest anywhere, not even in a place that offered great hope of success, till he had news of them' (Calvin).

*V*14: **But thanks be unto God, who always leadeth us in triumph in Christ, and maketh manifest through us the savour of his knowledge in every place.**

At this point Paul does not stop to explain how his anxiety was relieved by the coming of Titus [7.5ff], but immediately acknowledges his gratitude to God in a jubilant shout of praise. The figure is probably taken from a Roman triumph which the emperor would grant to a victorious general, the glory of whose conquests was also shared by his staff (cf F. F. Bruce: 'Now thanks to God, who always gives us a place of honour in Christ's triumphal procession').

The second part of the verse is an extension of the same image, for on such occasions the burning of incense carried the fragrance of victory far and wide. Thus Paul sees his apostolic progress through the world as a continuous triumph, by means of which the knowledge of Christ is spread abroad like perfume. As Christ's loyal lieutenant triumph is assured to Paul 'in every place', even at Corinth, the place where he had appeared to be facing an ignominious defeat!

V15: **For we are a sweet savour of Christ unto God, in them that are saved, and in them that perish; 16 to the one a savour from death unto death; to the other a savour from life unto life.**

As Paul is a chosen vessel filled with the fragrance of Christ, his preaching of the gospel is always a sweet savour to God, no matter whether men 'are being saved' through receiving it, or 'are perishing' in their rejection of it (ASV margin). The gospel divides mankind into two, and only two classes. In the one it is a fatal aroma that ends in death; in the other, a vital fragrance that leads to life. 'The Gospel is preached unto salvation, for that is its real purpose, but only believers share in this salvation; for unbelievers it is an occasion of condemnation, but it is they who make it so ... The proper function of the Gospel is always to be distinguished from what we may call its accidental function, which must be imputed to the depravity of men by which life is turned into death' (Calvin).

V16b: **And who is sufficient for these things? 17 For we are not as the many, corrupting the word of God: but as of sincerity, but as of God, in the sight of God, speak we in Christ.**

Since these momentous issues of life and death hang upon the preaching of the gospel, who is competent to exercise such a ministry? Who indeed, if not the apostle himself? [3.5]. Certainly not 'the many', those false apostles who sought to establish their own authority in the church at Corinth by disputing that of its founder (cf the 'some' of 3.1).

For we are not, like so many, peddlers of God's word; (RSV) Paul is adequate for the task, for he is not like those cheap-jacks who adulterate the Word of God and sell it for whatever price they can get. 'It is characteristic of these intruders that they go about hawking or peddling the word of God, cheapening and degrading the message by the illegitimate admixture of foreign elements, judaistic or pagan, as a dishonest merchant adulterates wine with water; they seek only their own gain, irrespective of the effect of their teaching on others and careless of the momentous issues which are at stake' (P. E. Hughes).

but as of sincerity, but as of God, in the sight of God, speak we in Christ. This 'completes the inward picture of Paul's preaching. His words spring not from selfish, but from genuine purposes, and from God; and are such words as men speak when sincere and when moved by God. They are spoken in the presence of God and in union with Christ as their encompassing element' (Beet).

CHAPTER THREE

*In claiming to be a competent minister of the gospel, Paul is not
commending himself, for he has no need of letters of commendation
when all men can read the living testimonial to his ministry in the
Corinthians themselves [vv 1–3]. It is God who has made him an
able minister of the new covenant, whose abiding glory far excels
the temporary splendour of that death-dealing ministry of condemnation which it has replaced [vv 4–11]. Unlike Moses who veiled
his face before the children of Israel, Paul delivers his message with
the openness and boldness that befits the greater light and liberty
which characterize the life-transforming dispensation of the Spirit
[vv 12–18].*

V1: **Are we beginning again to commend ourselves? or
need we, as do some, epistles of commendation to you
or from you?**

Are we beginning again to commend ourselves? In thus
protesting his sincerity [cf 2.17], Paul is well aware that his
opponents, whose calumnies had forced him to defend his
integrity [cf 5.12; ch 10–12], would say that he was again indulging a penchant for self-commendation [e.g. 1 *Cor* 4.16;
9.15; 14.18; 15.10].

**or need we, as do some, epistles of commendation to
you or from you?** But unlike 'some' (who belong to 'the

many' of 2.17), Paul does not think that those whom he has begotten through the gospel will suggest that he needs any introduction to them or any commendation from them [1 *Cor* 4.15]. These false teachers, however, had needed letters of commendation to gain access to the Corinthian church. And they would require similar letters on their departure from it, 'for they were largely dependent on these bills of clearance for profitable marketing of their merchandise in spiritual things' (P. E. Hughes). What Paul condemns is the unprincipled exploitation of this practice by these men; he has nothing to say against the usefulness of such letters in general [*Acts* 18.27; *Rom* 16.1; 1 *Cor* 16.3].

*V*2: **Ye are our epistle, written in our hearts, known and read of all men;**

If Paul has no need to flourish any testimonial that could be written with ink, it is because the Corinthians are his credentials. They themselves constitute the 'seal' of his apostleship [1 *Cor* 9.2]. This living letter is not only indelibly inscribed upon his heart [7.3], it is also *recognized* and *read* by everyone (Bruce). For though outsiders could not inspect Paul's heart, what Christ had written on their hearts through his ministry 'was patent to the world's observation, as it was reflected in their Christian mode of life' (J. H. Bernard). [*Matt* 5.14; *Rom* 1.8].

*V*3: **being made manifest that ye are an epistle of Christ, ministered by us, written not with ink, but with the Spirit of the living God; not in tables of stone, but in tables *that are* hearts of flesh.**

The Corinthians are indeed Paul's commendatory letter [*v* 2], but his part in their conversion was ministerial only. He claims to be no more than Christ's instrument. 'The Lord, so to speak, dictated the letter, and he wrote it. The contents of it were prescribed by Christ, and through the Apostle's ministry became visible and legible in the Corinthians' (J. Denney).

written not with ink, but with the Spirit of the living God; 'This "writing" which the Corinthians exhibit is no writing with ink on a papyrus roll, but is the mystical imprint of the Divine Spirit in their hearts, conveyed through Paul's ministrations' (Bernard).

not in tables of stone, but in tables *that are* hearts of flesh. The superiority of the new covenant over the old dispensation is not that it sets aside the decalogue (the moral law), but that it transfers that law from tables of stone to 'tables that are hearts of flesh' [cf *Ezek* 11.19; 36.26]. This is the fulfilment of Jeremiah's prophecy, 'I will put *my law* in their inward parts, and in their heart will I write it' [*Jer* 31.33]. If, as seems likely, Paul's opponents in Corinth were Judaizers who gloried in the law ('ministers of righteousness' 11.15), it is easy to see how the argument of this chapter would fall upon them with overwhelming force. It is certain that the original apostles did not endorse this teaching with letters of commendation, but their continued observance of the *ceremonial* law led the Judaizers to suppose 'that legalism was of the essence of their religion' (J. G. Machen cited by Plummer).

*V*4: **And such confidence have we through Christ to God-ward: 5 not that we are sufficient of ourselves, to account anything as from ourselves; but our sufficiency is from God;**

Thus Paul is confident that his work in Corinth is a standing testimony to the reality of his divine commission. 'This confidence is not mere self-assumption, but a firm assurance, reaching through Christ to the presence of God, and therefore valid in the sight of the searcher of hearts' (J. Waite). But to obviate the charge of boasting Paul clearly disclaims any credit for the gracious work that was done in Corinth, for in and of himself he was quite unequal to the task. The secret of his successful ministry there is not to be found in any natural competence, but solely in the sufficiency of the God who called and equipped him for it [1 Cor 15.10; cf 4.7].

V6: **who also made us sufficient as ministers of a new covenant; not of the letter, but of the spirit: for the letter killeth, but the spirit giveth life.**

Instead of believing the empty claims of the false apostles, the Corinthians should be the first to acknowledge that Paul has a valid and effective ministry. It is *valid* because he did not appoint himself to it, but can point to the particular occasion when God's commission made him sufficient for it [Acts 9.3ff; 22.12ff; 26.15–18]. It is *effective* because it is the ministry of a new covenant. The very provision of a fresh covenant indicates its superiority over the worn out and obsolete dispensation which it replaces [Heb 8.6–13]. This covenant is not a mutual compact between equals, but a 'unilateral enactment' of which God is the sovereign disposer; and its uniqueness lies in the accomplishing of that which the law demanded but gave no power to perform.

not of the letter, but of the spirit: for the letter killeth, but the spirit giveth life. The law of God externally engraved on tables of stone is here adversely compared with that same law internally inscribed in the heart of the believer. Sinners confronted by a condemning code could only be killed by it, but the spiritual application of a fulfilled law confers life. Paul neither depreciates the law nor contradicts its plain meaning; he is showing that the natural man's inability to obey it must result in death [Rom 6.23; 7.6–12; Gal 3.10]. The grace of the new covenant 'is life-giving, in that Christ, who as God is the law-giver and as Man is the *only* law-keeper, vicariously endured the sinner's death penalty, ridding us, as it were, of the legal document with its accusing ordinances and nailing it to His cross for all to see [Col 2.14f], and also, by the Pentecostal outpouring of the Holy Spirit, communicated His life and obedience to every trusting heart' (P. E. Hughes).

*V*7: **But if the ministration of death, written, *and* engraven on stones, came with glory, so that the children of Israel could not look steadfastly upon the face of Moses for the glory of his face; which *glory* was passing away: 8 how shall not rather the ministration of the spirit be with glory?**

As Moses descended from the mount his face shone with a glory that testified to the divine origin of the covenant of which he was the mediator, yet death was the unavoidable result of a ministry whose content was only 'engraved in letters on stones' (Lenski). [Exod 34.29–35] But though the ministration of condemnation was so gloriously inaugurated, the fading of this radiance from the face of Moses showed that its glory 'was being done away' (ASV margin). For God always intended to replace it with the abiding and far more resplendent ministration of the spirit. Nevertheless it is the function of the law to convict men of their sin and drive them to faith in the promise [Gal 3.24, 25]. Consequently even the Old Testament saints were saved by their faith in the promise, and not by their obedience to the law [Rom 4.1–8]. For 'by the works of the law shall no flesh be justified in his sight' [Rom 3.20; Gal 2.16]. In effect Paul warns the Corinthians that to give heed to Judaizers who exalt the law at the expense

[43]

of the gospel is to turn away from that salvation which is theirs by grace through faith alone.

*V*9: **For if the ministration of condemnation hath glory, much rather doth the ministration of righteousness exceed in glory.**

The ministration of righteousness abounds with greater glory than that which attended the ministry of condemnation, for it is a greater matter to secure the justification of a sinner than to confirm his condemnation. It takes only the letter of the law on slabs of stone to condemn him, but it required the blood of God's own Son and the Spirit's quickening power to make him an heir of an everlasting righteousness [cf 5.21; *Rom* 3.19–26; 8.16ff; 1 *Cor* 1.30].

*V*10: **For verily that which hath been made glorious hath not been made glorious in this respect, by reason of the glory that surpasseth.**

Although the ministration of the old covenant was truly glorious, yet this seemed as nothing in comparison with the transcendent glory of the new covenant. 'Just as the moon and the stars, though they are themselves bright and spread their light over all the earth, yet vanish before the greater brightness of the sun, so the Law, however glorious in itself, has no glory in face of the Gospel's grandeur' (Calvin).

*V*11: **For if that which passeth away *was* with glory, much more that which remaineth *is* in glory.**

At Sinai the old covenant came *with* glory; the new abides *in* glory as its distinctive element. 'The old dispensation and its ministry were temporary, the new is permanent. There is nothing to intervene, no new revelation, no new economy, between the gospel and its ministry, and the final consummation. Whoever are to be converted, whatever nations are to be brought in, it must be by the preaching of the gospel, "which remaineth," or is to continue, according to Christ's promise, until the end of the world' (Hodge).

*V*12: **Having therefore such a hope, we use great boldness of speech,**

Since Paul has a sure hope that the glory of the new covenant will abide forever [*v* 11], he uses great boldness of speech. For now the full openness of the gospel has superseded the comparative obscurity of the preparatory dispensation. Therefore the unreserved frankness with which he glorifies his ministry is entirely appropriate, even though some should mistake it for self-commendation [*v* 1]. This 'boldness' or 'openness' of speech that characterizes Paul's ministry stems from the liberty of access to God which he enjoys through Christ [*v* 18]. 'He who lifts up his face uncovered to God also turns uncovered to men ... The apostle can lift up his face openly to God and men because he serves incorruptible *glory* and kindles unshakeable hope, 3.7ff.' (H. Schlier, *TDNT*, Vol. V, p. 883).

*V*13: **and *are* not as Moses, *who* put a veil upon his face, that the children of Israel should not look steadfastly on the end of that which was passing away:**

As the minister of a covenant whose glory can never be dimmed, it is not for Paul to do as Moses did [*Exod* 34.33–35 RV]. For after Moses had spoken the words of God to the people it was his custom to cover his face with a veil, which meant that the Israelites could not even look upon the reflected glory of a vanishing order without concealment. But as the revelation vouchsafed to Paul can never be suspended or superseded, no such intervening veil obscures the abiding glory of the gospel. 'His is not a message of condemnation and death, but of grace and mercy and life to every sinner who repents and believes. The eye of faith may gaze upon the everlasting glory of Christ without interruption' (P. E. Hughes).

*V*14: **but their minds were hardened: for until this very day at the reading of the old covenant the same veil remaineth, it not being revealed *to them* that it is done away in Christ.**

But their minds were blinded: (AV). 'Hardened' is a misleading rendering when 'intellectual obtuseness or blindness is the sense which is most appropriate to this context' (J. Armitage Robinson, p. 265). Thus the veil which hid the face of Moses answered to the spiritual insensibility of those to whom he ministered [*Deut* 29.4]. 'Unless God give sight as well as light, and enlighten both organ and object, we can see nothing' (John Trapp).

for to this day, when they read the old covenant, that same veil remains unlifted, because only through Christ is it taken away. (RSV) This translation is preferable to the less likely alternative which is mentioned in the RV margin and adopted in the ASV text. Paul is saying that the same veil of unbelief prevents the Jews of his day from understanding the real significance of the revelation which was given to them through Moses. For it is only by receiving the One of whom Moses spoke that this veil can ever be removed [*John* 5.46]. 'The Old Testament Scriptures are intelligible only when understood as predicting and prefiguring Christ' (Hodge). [*Luke* 24.44ff] The expression, 'old covenant', occurs only here in the New Testament and Paul may well have coined it as a counterpart to the 'new covenant' which Christ inaugurated by his death, cf 1 *Cor* 11.25 (so H. Seesemann,

TDNT, Vol. V, p. 720). That Paul could so refer to the religion of his own early manhood as the 'worn out' (*palaios*)
covenant affords striking evidence of how completely he dis-
sociated Judaism from Christianity, especially when it is re-
membered that it had been replaced by the new [*kainos*: cf
v 6] covenant only thirty years before he wrote this letter (so
Bernard). [*Acts* 13.19; *Rom* 10.1ff; *Phil* 3.3ff]

V15: **But unto this day, whensoever Moses is read, a
veil lieth upon their heart.**

The thought of the previous verse is here carried to its climax.
As the veil over Moses' face concealed the passing glory of
the old covenant from the children of Israel, so today their
descendants fail to understand the Book of Moses, even though
it is read to them every Sabbath [*Acts* 15.21]. 'Like its author
at Sinai, the book is veiled. Or, rather, on the readers' hearts
a veil lies. For the hindrance is in themselves' (Beet).

V16: **But whensoever it shall turn to the Lord, the veil
is taken away.**

As the subject of the verb 'turn' is unexpressed, 'it' could refer
to 'their heart' [*v* 15], 'Israel', or 'anyone'. Paul probably
means 'anyone' i.e. any Jew, for he is here drawing a general
principle from *Exod* 34.34, which says that whenever Moses
'went in before Jehovah to speak with him, he took the veil
off.' In the same way, whenever a Jew turns to Christ, the
veil is taken away; because it is 'only through Christ' [*v* 14],
the fulfiller of the law [*Rom* 10.4], that the impediment of the
legal dispensation is removed.

V17: **Now the Lord is the Spirit: and where the Spirit
of the Lord is, *there* is liberty.**

Now the 'Lord' means the 'Spirit': (Bruce) Paul now explains that in this new era of grace, 'the Lord' (i.e. Jehovah, *v* 16) whom Moses approached corresponds to the life-giving 'Spirit', who enables us Christians to enter the divine presence 'with unveiled face' [*v* 18]'. Although some have claimed that the apostle here virtually identifies the exalted Christ with the Holy Spirit, he is not in fact confusing the distinct identity of their persons, but is stressing the unity of their work in the economy of redemption. For as every genuine experience of the Spirit must lead to the confession 'Jesus is Lord' [1 *Cor* 12.3], so here Paul insists 'that what the Spirit does is exactly what the Lord does; the Spirit's work is not an additional or special work *beyond* the the Lord's; the Spirit *is* the Lord at work' (F. D. Bruner, *A Theology of the Holy Spirit,* p. 289). [cf *John* 16.12–16].

and where the Spirit of the Lord is, *there* **is liberty.** It is always and only by his Spirit that Christ communicates to men the liberty he died to secure, so that whenever he removes the veil of unbelief from their hearts the bondage of the law gives way to the freedom of the gospel [*John* 8.36, 39; *Rom* 8.15; *Gal* 5.1].

*V*18: **But we all, with unveiled face beholding as in a mirror the glory of the Lord, are transformed into the same image from glory to glory, even as from the Lord the Spirit.**

Whereas Moses alone was privileged to behold the glory of God with unveiled face, now all Christians may always gaze directly upon the full revelation of that glory 'in the face of Jesus Christ' [4.6]. 'We are transformed into the image of the Lord by beholding it, not by reflecting it. The common interpretation is therefore to be preferred; *beholding as in a mirror*. Though in comparison with the unconverted those who are turned to the Lord see clearly, or with an unveiled face, still it is only as in a mirror. 1 *Cor* 13.12. It is not the immediate, beatific vision of the glory of the Lord, which is only enjoyed in heaven, but it is that manifestation of his glory which is made in his word and by his Spirit, whose office it is to glorify Christ by revealing him to us. *John* 16.14' (Hodge).

are transformed into the same image from glory to glory, This transformation of believers already begins in their present life on earth. As they behold the heavenly glory of Christ in the mirror of his Word, they are progressively changed 'into the same image', and this process of inward renewal issues in the outward refashioning of the life [*Rom* 12.2]. There is no thought here of mystical deification, for the change into the likeness of Christ is the restoration of the divine image in man at creation, 'and it maintains the characteristically biblical distance between God and man. The initiate has no aristocratic claim to a special experience of God; all Christians participate in the miracle of transformation' (J. Behm, *TDNT*, Vol. IV, pp. 758–759).

even as from the Lord the Spirit. Since such an amazing change clearly demands the exercise of supernatural power, Paul attributes it to the Lord who is the Spirit, and thereby rejects that spurious spirituality which would sever the work of the Spirit from the Lord, whose mission he fulfils in the world [*v* 17]. 'Our whole transformation is the work of the Lord in and by and through the Spirit. All Scripture agrees in regard to that' (Lenski).

CHAPTER FOUR

As a minister of the new covenant, Paul has renounced all dishonesty and deceit, and commends himself to every man's conscience by openly proclaiming the truth [vv 1–2]. So if his gospel remains veiled, it is because the god of this world has blinded the minds of the unbelieving, that they might not see the glory of Christ who is the image of God [vv 3–4]. We preach not ourselves but Christ, for God who brought light out of darkness, has illuminated our hearts with the knowledge of his glory in the face of Christ [vv 5–6]. But we have this treasure in earthen vessels to show that its power is of God [v 7]. It is through the risen life of Jesus that Paul's afflictions benefit the Corinthians, for the death which is at work in him brings life to them [vv 8–12]. He is sustained in these sufferings by the knowledge that he is being inwardly renewed day by day, and by the assurance that his light affliction will lead to an eternal weight of glory [vv 13–17]. Hence he looks not at the temporal things which are seen, but at the invisible realities which are eternal [v 18].

V1: **Therefore seeing we have this ministry, even as we obtained mercy, we faint not:**

It is not in any spirit of self-sufficiency, but with a lively sense of the distinguishing mercy of God in granting this glorious ministry of the new covenant to one who 'was before a blasphemer and a persecutor', that Paul continues faithfully to discharge it despite all discouragement [*Exod* 33.19; 1 *Tim* 1. 12–16]. As the unworthy recipient of such mercy and such a ministry he does not lose heart, remaining resolute in his re-fusal to compromise the truth of the gospel to suit Jewish pre-judice [*vv* 2ff; *Gal* 5.11; 6.12].

*V*2: **but we have renounced the hidden things of shame, not walking in craftiness, nor handling the word of God deceitfully; but by the manifestation of the truth com-mending ourselves to every man's conscience in the sight of God.**

But we have renounced the things that are hidden out of a sense of shame, (Arndt-Gingrich). As befits the openness of his ministry, Paul has refused to adopt the tactics of the false apostles who gain their converts by guile, and who try to hide their shame by accusing him of the very things of which they themselves are guilty [12.16].

not walking in craftiness, nor handling the word of God deceitfully; The apostle plainly contrasts the purity of his own conduct and his honest proclamation of the Word of God with the deceitful practice of these interlopers who rob-bed the gospel of its power to save by their adulteration of its content in order to enrich themselves [2.17].

but by the manifestation of the truth commending our-selves to every man's conscience. On the contrary, Paul's ministry is marked by 'the open proclamation of the truth' (Arndt-Gingrich), and it is solely by this transparent fidelity to 'the whole counsel of God' that he expects to commend himself (lit.) 'to every conscience of men'. For he is confident that the truth, the whole truth, and nothing but the truth, must find an answering echo in every conscience, even if it be sinfully suppressed by many.

in the sight of God. This is added 'because conscience holds us accountable to God. Drop the idea of God, and the vitality of conscience is destroyed. Mere abstract ideas of "right" and "wrong" do not bind the conscience; the idea of God and his judgment does' (Lenski). [1.12; 2.17]

*V*3: **And even if our gospel is veiled, it is veiled in them that perish:**

In spite of the apostle's claim to preach the truth openly [*v* 2], it seems that his opponents in Corinth had said that his message was hopelessly obscure [cf 2 *Pet* 3.16]. If, however, Paul's gospel is veiled, the fault lies not in the obscurity of his preaching, but in the spiritual blindness of those who are on the high road to perdition (ASV margin: 'it is veiled in them that are perishing'). 'Those from whom it is hidden must therefore be blind and lacking in every trace of rational under-standing. The conclusion is that the blindness of unbelievers in no way detracts from the clarity of his Gospel; the sun is no less bright because blind men do not perceive its light' (Calvin).

*V*4: **in whom the god of this world hath blinded the minds of the unbelieving, that the light of the gospel of the glory of Christ, who is the image of God, should not dawn** *upon them.*

in whom the god of this age hath blinded the minds of the unbelieving, (ASV margin) It is because Satan has blinded their minds that those who are perishing do not believe the only Word that could save them. And it is by this blinding of the mind that Satan has secured their vassalage to himself as 'the god of this age', though, as dependent creatures, neither he nor they ever succeed in escaping from the lordship and judgment of the one living and true God. As Trapp observes, 'The devil usurps such a power, and wicked men will have it so ... Their buildings, ploughings, plantings, sailings, are for the devil. And if we could rip up their hearts, we should find written therein, The god of this present world' [cf *John* 12.31; 16.11; *Eph* 2.2; 1 *John* 5.19].

that they should not see the light of the gospel of the glory of Christ, (ASV margin) Unlike the message peddled by the Judaizers, Paul's gospel is a revelation of the glory of Christ [*Acts* 26.13–18]. 'To see this glory is to be saved; for we are thereby transformed into his likeness from glory to glory, 3.18. Therefore it is that Satan, the great adversary, directs all his energy to prevent men becoming the subjects of that illumination of which the gospel, as the revelation of the glory of Christ, is the source' (Hodge).

who is the image of God. This is the supreme climax. Paul here comes near to the teaching of the Fourth Gospel [*John* 1.18]. What he affirms is not Christ's likeness to the Father, but his essential oneness with the Father. 'He who sees the Son, sees the Father, *in the face* of Christ. The Son exactly represents and reflects the Father' (J. A. Bengel). [*v* 6; *Col* 1.15; *John* 14.9; *Heb* 1.3)

V5: **For we preach not ourselves, but Christ Jesus as Lord, and ourselves as your servants for Jesus' sake.**

Since Paul was commissioned to preach a gospel which has the glory of Christ for its content, he does not preach himself, as his opponents allege, but Christ Jesus as Lord. Hence those who reject his preaching, repudiate not the preacher but the Christ he preaches. 'To "preach Christ as Lord" is to preach Him as crucified, risen, and glorified, the Lord to whom "all authority in heaven and earth has been given." To confess Him as Lord is to declare oneself a Christian [*Rom* 10.9; 1 *Cor* 12.3]' (Plummer).

and ourselves as your servants for Jesus' sake. Far from claiming any lordship over their faith [1.24], Paul presents himself as their bondservant for the sake of the one Master who took upon him 'the form of a servant' [*Phil* 2.7]. Thus though he is their minister, they are not his masters [1 *Cor* 7.23]. 'The ideal of a Christian minister, as presented in this pregnant passage, is, that he is a preacher of Christ, and a servant of the church, governed and animated by the love of Jesus' (Hodge).

V6: **Seeing it is God, that said, Light shall shine out of darkness, who shined in our hearts, to give the light of the knowledge of the glory of God in the face of Jesus Christ.**

Paul cannot but preach Christ, for God whose first creative word brought light out of darkness [Gen 1.3], is he who shone into his heart in re-creating grace [5.17]. As this spiritual experience is common to all Christians, Paul here stresses the subjective effect of this ('in our hearts') instead of dwelling upon the objective vision of Christ by which it was produced in him [1 *Cor* 9.1]. 'For as in His creation of the world God has poured forth upon us the brightness of the sun and has also given us eyes with which to receive it, so in our redemption He shines forth upon us in the person of His Son by His Gospel, but that would be in vain, since we are blind, unless He were also to illuminate our minds by His Spirit' (Calvin).

Moreover, it is only because Paul has been divinely illuminated himself that he can be used by God to turn men 'from darkness to light' [*Acts* 26.18]. For those whose spiritual eyes are still covered by the scales of unbelief obviously cannot reveal Christ to others [cf *Acts* 9.18]. Although Paul impinges on Hellenistic mysticism in linking God, light, and saving knowledge, he diverges from it in that he does not think in terms of a mystical union and inner light, but primarily in terms of an historical act of salvation and the knowledge bound up with it, 'which is then used by God for missionary transmission' (so A. Oepke, *TDNT*, Vol. IV, p. 26).

*V*7: **But we have this treasure in earthen vessels, that the exceeding greatness of the power may be of God, and not from ourselves;**

After Paul has spoken so exultingly of 'the light of the knowledge of the glory of God' [*v* 6], it is surprising to find that this treasure is placed in such mean and perishable vessels. The 'majesty of the message is in strange contrast with the weak and buffeted and fragile person of the messenger' (Allan Menzies). The amazing effects produced by the possession of this divine knowledge are evidently 'beyond all measure and proportion' to the means used to diffuse it (Arndt-Gingrich). For it is God's purpose to show that this power cannot be ascribed to the weak vessels in which it is contained, but that it belongs continually to him from whom it comes.

*V*8: *we are* **pressed on every side, yet not straitened; perplexed, yet not unto despair;** 9 **pursued, yet not forsaken; smitten down, yet not destroyed;**

Paul's constant experience as a minister of Christ is now illustrated in a vivid metaphor, expressed in four pairs of participles which form a climax. 'The first clause in each member of the series implies the *earthiness of the vessels,* the second clause the *excellency of the power*' (Fausset).

[55]

1. **In every direction pressed hard, but not hemmed in;** (Bernard) The apostle thinks of himself as a combatant engaged by an apparently stronger foe whose persistent attacks leave him no room to manoeuvre, yet God does not suffer him to be crushed into a corner [1 *Cor* 10.13].

2. **bewildered, but not utterly despairing;** (Bernard) Or preserving the play on words: 'confused, but not confounded' (P. E. Hughes). He is often perplexed by the crafty stratagems of his adversary, but God does not permit him to be reduced to blank despair [1.8–10; 7.5ff].

3. **pursued, but not forsaken** (i.e. abandoned to the pursuing foe); (Bernard) Although he is hunted by a killer intent on dealing him the death-blow, he is not deserted by God in his extremity [*Josh* 1.5].

4. **struck down** (as by an arrow), **but not destroyed;** (Bernard) And even when he is felled by what his enemy takes to be the final stroke, the unexpected power of God ensures that he is far from finished [11.23; *Acts* 14.19f].

*V*10: **always bearing about in the body the dying of Jesus, that the life also of Jesus may be manifested in our body.**

This sums up and explains the significance of Paul's afflictions [*vv* 8, 9]. Here his choice of the word which points to the process of dying (lit. 'the putting to death') shows that the sufferings of Jesus are of necessity reproduced in his apostle [cf *Acts* 9.16; 14.22]. His devotion to Jesus is the magnet that irresistibly draws the world's hostility upon himself [*Gal* 6.17]. For the same enmity which reached its culmination in the crucifixion of Jesus now pursues those whom he has chosen out of the world [*John* 15.18–21]. The verse shows that Paul 'taught his converts details in the history of Jesus, especially His sufferings ending in death. Here he assumes that they know' (Plummer).

that the life also of Jesus may be manifested in our body. This discloses the purpose of these sufferings. Paul bears about the *dying* of Jesus in order that the *life* also of Jesus may be manifested in his body. For the inextinguishable resurrection-life of the Jesus who once died is demonstrated in his many deliverances from the jaws of death. It is evident that the distinction made by liberal theologians between the 'Jesus of history' and the 'Christ of faith' was quite foreign to Paul's thought. He 'does not separate the historic Jesus from the glorified Christ. To him it is the same Jesus' (Plummer).

*V*11: **For we who live are always delivered unto death for Jesus' sake, that the life also of Jesus may be manifested in our mortal flesh.**

Several new elements appear in this explanatory re-statement of the previous verse. 1. It is because Paul is a 'living one', i.e. one whose essential life is the eternal life of Jesus, that the deaths to which he is always being handed over serve to exhibit the triumph of that divine life. 2. The sphere in which this resurrection-life of Jesus is displayed is a body of 'mortal flesh', i.e. a body in subjection to the power of death. 'Christ's followers are in this life delivered unto death, that His life may be manifested in that which naturally is the seat of decay and death. That which is subject to suffering is that in which the power of Him who suffered here is most manifested' (W. E. Vine). 3. 'It is for Jesus' sake – because of Jesus – that he suffers. It is only suffering of this kind, which is so abundantly blessed' (H. L. Goudge).

V12: **So then death worketh in us, but life in you.**

A new contrast is brought out by another bold paradox, which links Paul's present theme of 'dying yet living' with the earlier reference to his sufferings in Chapter 1.4–7. Although he knows that death is already at work in him, he is comforted by the fact that his *physical* sufferings have been fruitful in bringing *spiritual* life to the Corinthians. The apostle thus saw his afflictions as directly contributing to the enrichment of his converts. As a herald of the cross he was glad to accept more than his fair share of suffering in order to benefit them [1.6; *Col* 1.24].

V13: **But having the same spirit of faith, according to that which is written, I believed, and therefore did I speak; we also believe, and therefore also we speak;**

Since Paul has the same spirit of faith as David had in similar straits ('I believed, and therefore did I speak': *Ps* 116.10 LXX), he also believes and continues to declare his faith, even though death should soon silence his testimony to the truth [cf *Acts* 4.20]. This means that Paul and David share the same objective faith. For both Testaments contain the same truth, the Old in the form of promise, the New in the form of fulfilment. 'Hence the spirit of both is identical in defying persecution and death' (Lenski).

V14: **knowing that he that raised up the Lord Jesus shall raise up us also with Jesus, and shall present us with you.**

Paul is fearless in the face of death because he knows that God who raised up the Lord Jesus 'shall raise up us also *with* Jesus'. This obviously does not mean at the same time as Jesus, but in virtue of our union with him. For there could be no resurrection of believers apart from his triumph over death [1 *Cor*

15.23]. And God will raise up Paul together with the believers in Corinth ('us with you') in order to present them 'before the presence of his glory with exceeding joy' [*Col* 1.22; *Eph* 5.27; *Jude* 24].

As Paul here speaks of being raised from the dead, some have maintained that this represents a change in his eschatological expectations [cf 1 *Thess* 4.15, 17]. Yet it is a mistake to assume that the exhortation to live in the light of the imminent (but not *immediate*: cf 2 *Thess* 2.2; 3.5] return of Christ was based on a categorical assurance that either he or his first readers (in Thessalonica, or elsewhere) would be alive when that event took place. In this respect Paul knew no more than we do ourselves today, for neither the time of his death nor the date of the Parousia was revealed to him [*Matt* 24.36].

*V*15: **For all things *are* for your sakes, that the grace, being multiplied through the many, may cause the thanksgiving to abound unto the glory of God.**

Paul concludes the paragraph by saying that the proximate end of his sufferings [*vv* 7–13] is the salvation of the Corinthians, while the ultimate result is the glory of God. For 'the more people who come to know the grace of God through the gospel Paul preaches, the more numerous will be the thanksgiving that will be evoked, and the greater the praise that will be offered to God' (R. V. G. Tasker).

*V*16: **Wherefore we faint not; but though our outward man is decaying, yet our inward man is renewed day by day.**

Wherefore we faint not; This looks back to verse 1. As the minister of a new and superior covenant, who is sustained in all his trials by the hope of the glory to come [*vv* 14, 15], it is no wonder that Paul does not lose heart.

[59]

but though our outward man is decaying, yet our inward man is renewed day by day. As the contrast Paul makes here is between the declining powers of his bodily life and the progressive renewal of his spiritual life, the 'outward man' must not be confused with the unregenerate 'old man' of *Rom* 6.6; *Eph* 4.22 and *Col* 3.9. It is evident that the apostle's afflictions have hastened that process of decay to which his physical life, as at present constituted, is subject. This necessarily includes every faculty which depends upon the body for its proper functioning. On the other hand, what he most essentially *is* by regenerating grace cannot be destroyed, but is being renewed day by day [3.18]. 'The decay of the outward man in the godless is a melancholy spectacle, for it is the decay of everything; in the Christian it does not touch that life which is hid with Christ in God, and which is in the soul itself a well of water springing up to life eternal' (Denney). [*John* 4.14; *Col* 3.3]

*V*17: **For our light affliction, which is for the moment, worketh for us more and more exceedingly an eternal weight of glory;**

As the verb 'worketh' also means 'earns', Roman Catholic expositors use the verse as a text on which to hang their doctrine of merit. But though God makes present afflictions the means of obtaining future glory, it is false to infer that they are the meritorious cause of it. 'The spirit of faith which realizes the substance of things not seen inverts the usual relation of ideas. Affliction, generally regarded as a load, has here the quality of lightness. Glory, generally regarded as an ethereal splendour, is a weight. The affliction is not light in itself, but only when put in the balance with the weight, nor momentary in itself, but only when set against eternity . . . The idea in the apostle's mind is that the sufferings of Christ borne by his ministers and followers lead them to glory, even as they led

Christ himself to glory, because they are always accompanied by rich supplies of the Spirit and life' (Waite). [*Rom* 8.17, 18]

*V*18: **while we look not at the things which are seen, but at the things which are not seen: for the things which are seen are temporal; but the things which are not seen are eternal.**

Meanwhile Paul fixes his gaze, not on the things seen, but on the things not seen: for the things which are visible to the eye of sense are transient, but the realities which as yet can only be discerned by the eye of faith are eternal [*Col* 3.1–4]. 'Note well what it is that will make all the miseries of this world easy to endure; it is that we should transfer our thoughts to the eternity of the kingdom of heaven. If we look around us, a moment can seem a long time, but when we lift up our hearts heavenwards, a thousand years begin to be like a moment' (Calvin).

CHAPTER FIVE

Paul does not lose heart in the midst of his sufferings, because he knows that if death destroys his earthly tent, he has the certainty of receiving from God an eternal, heavenly house at the resurrection [v 1]. For in this weak earthly body he groans for the glory to come; not that he wished to be found in a disembodied state, but rather to be clothed with his heavenly body so that mortality might be swallowed up in life [vv 2–4]. He owes this confidence to God who gave him the Holy Spirit as the pledge of his glorification [v 5]. So he is always of good courage, and since he walks by faith and not by sight, he would rather be present with the Lord even if this means absence from the body [vv 6–8]. Paul therefore always aims to please Christ, before whose tribunal all men must at last appear, in order that each may be judged according to his deeds [vv 9, 10]. With that awesome day in view, he faithfully discharges his commission. In saying this he commends not himself, but gives the Corinthians the opportunity to answer those who glory in appearance and not in heart [vv 11, 12]. Whether or not Paul is beside himself, he obeys God in order to benefit them. For the love of Christ constrains him, because he judges that those for whom Christ died should not henceforth live unto themselves, but unto him who for their sakes died and rose again [vv 13–15]. Consequently, he no longer knows any man after the flesh, even though he had once thought of Christ in this worldly way. For if any man is in Christ, there is a new creation, and the old life is displaced by the new [vv 16, 17]. All this is of God, who reconciled us to himself through

Christ, and gave us the ministry of reconciliation; namely, that God was reconciling the world unto himself in Christ, not counting their trespasses against them [vv 18, 19]. As an ambassador for Christ, Paul therefore beseeches men to be reconciled to God. For God made him who knew no sin to be sin for us, that we might become the righteousness of God in him [vv 20, 21].

V1: **For we know that if the earthly house of our tabernacle be dissolved, we have a building from God, a house not made with hands, eternal, in the heavens.**

For we know that Paul is lifted above earthly affliction by this heavenly hope [4.17, 18]. For he knows by immediate revelation, as the Corinthians also know because he had taught it them [1 *Cor* 15], that if the frail tent in which they live their earthly life is dismantled by death, they have the assurance of receiving from God an eternal and heavenly house. It is only the certainty of this resurrection of the body to life eternal that enables him to contemplate its dissolution with composure.

if But though Paul is content to die [vv 6–8], he still says 'if' and not 'when', for in the event of Christ's prior return he would not experience death, but instantaneous glorification as in 1 *Cor* 15.51 (see also comment on 4.14).

the earthly tent we live in is taken down, (Arndt-Gingrich) A natural image for an itinerant tentmaker [*Acts* 18.3] to use to describe the inferior, insecure, and impermanent nature of the present life. Although recent afflictions [1.8] had made the apostle acutely aware that his 'earthly tent' was being destroyed [4.16], his daily inward renewal by the Spirit was the pledge of its replacement by a glorious and eternal edifice [cf *Rom* 8.11].

we have The present tense expresses the certainty of our possessing it, and must not be pressed to suggest 'the mechanical theory that the body of glory exists *now* in heaven, in an organic form' (Waite).

a building from God, a house not made with hands, eternal, Since Paul speaks of this body as a building, he appropriately uses the expression 'not made with hands' to point to its divine origin [cf *Col* 2.11; *Heb* 9.11]. It is the *direct* creation of God, an eternal building as contrasted with a perishable tent. This usage makes it appear certain that Paul knew of the charge that was brought against the Lord, that he would destroy the temple made with hands, and in three days build another 'not made with hands' [*Mark* 14.58; cf *John* 2.19–21].

in the heavens. 'It is practically in heaven: for the power which will raise it is there. When Christ appears from heaven we shall receive our permanent bodily abode. Hence it is also "our dwelling place from heaven", *v* 2. Consequently, this building is completely beyond the reach of the uncertainties of earth' (Beet).

V2: **For verily in this we groan, longing to be clothed upon with our habitation which is from heaven:**

For in this earthly tent which is our mortal body, we groan for the glory to come [*Rom* 8.19–23; *Phil* 3.20, 21]. Paul longs to be set free from the sufferings and imperfections of this present life, and to have his heavenly habitation 'put on over' his earthly body, 'so that there shall be transformation [1 *Cor* 15.51f], not death' (J. Massie).

which is from heaven: The distinguishing properties of the resurrection-body will flow from 'that resurrection-life which resides in "the Lord from heaven". And, as Bengel says, if it

be "*from* heaven", the thing meant cannot be heaven itself'
(David Brown).

V3: **if so be that being clothed we shall not be found
naked.**

**inasmuch as we, having put it on, shall not be found
naked.** (Arndt-Gingrich) This clarifies and confirms the
meaning of the previous verse. If Paul is still clothed with his
natural body at the Lord's appearing, he will avoid the nakedness of the disembodied state. For then 'his assumption of the
new body will be a superinvestment, a process like that of
putting on an upper garment' (Waite).

The statement would also have special point for those in
Corinth who denied the resurrection of the body [1 *Cor*
15.12]. These 'gnostics' maintained that the resurrection was
past already, apparently claiming that they had experienced it
in conversion or baptism [2 *Tim* 2.17, 18]. But to Paul who
made no dualistic distinction between the soul and the body,
such a bodiless existence held no attractions, and he implicitly condemns this denial of the Christian hope by describing
it as a condition of 'nakedness'.

V4: **For indeed we that are in this tabernacle do groan,
being burdened; not for that we would be unclothed,
but that we would be clothed upon, that what is mortal
may be swallowed up of life.**

The burden under which Paul groans is not the mere fear of
death, but the separation of the body from the soul by death.
Because death is the unnatural disruption of man's being as
created by God, he could never be satisfied with a gospel
which only provided for the redemption of the soul. He longs
for something far richer than the bodiless survival of the soul
after death. What therefore concerns him is whether he will

have to face 'a *protracted* state of being unclothed, that is "naked" between his possible death and the arrival of the parousia' (Geerhardus Vos). For he cannot regard his salvation as complete until he is clothed with the resurrection-body of glory. Thus Paul would prefer to be alive at Christ's coming so that 'what is mortal', i.e. his present mortal body, might immediately be transformed into the body of glory [1 *Cor* 15.53, 54].

V5: **Now he that wrought us for this very thing is God, who gave unto us the earnest of the Spirit.**

It is God who prepared us 'for this very thing', the transformation of the body [*v* 4], by the gift of the Holy Spirit whose present transforming work within [3.18; 4.16] is the pledge or first instalment of the glory to come [1.22; *Eph* 1.14). Thus 'the present possession of the Spirit is regarded in the light of an anticipation. The Spirit's proper sphere is the future aeon; from thence He projects Himself into the present, and becomes a prophecy of Himself in his eschatological operations' (Vos).

V6: **Being therefore always of good courage, and knowing that, whilst we are at home in the body, we are absent from the Lord**

Since God has guaranteed the future [*v* 5], Paul is always of good courage, despite his uncertainty as to whether he will live to see the Lord's return; for his dread of being unclothed by death is offset by the knowledge that as long as he is at home in the body, he is away from his glorified Lord in heaven. For though Christ is always spiritually present with his people [*Matt* 28.20], they do not enjoy his bodily presence while they remain on earth [*Acts* 3.21]. Now 'He does not show Himself to us face to face, because we are still exiles from His Kingdom and do not yet possess that blessed immortality that the angels who are with Him enjoy' (Calvin).

*V*7: **(for we walk by faith, not by sight);**

The parenthesis explains the sense in which Paul is 'absent from the Lord'. For while he is at home in the body, the region 'through which he walks is one in which the heavenly things gazed upon are not seen in their actual substance, but only realized, as far as that is possible, by the spiritual discernment of faith [*Heb* 11.1]. When he migrates to the Lord, he enjoys the sight of the things themselves' (Waite).

*V*8: **we are of good courage, I say, and are willing rather to be absent from the body, and to be at home with the Lord.**

As Paul was unsure of what was in store for him, he could not count on being alive at the parousia. 'Therefore he says only as much as he could with full certainty profess: to be absent from the body is to be at home with the Lord. Even in case that happened which appeared to him the less desirable, he would still be contented, because in this being with the Lord everything else was potentially given' (Vos). [cf *Phil* 1.21–23]

*V*9: **Wherefore also we make it our aim, whether at home or absent, to be well-pleasing unto him.**

Whether therefore Paul is in the body or out of it at the Lord's return, his constant ambition, and the only lawful one (Bengel), is to win his approval. For whatever the Lord's appointment for him may be, whether it be life or death, his absolute commitment to Christ remains the same [*Rom* 14.8; *Phil* 1.20; 1 *Thess* 5.10].

*V*10: **For we must all be made manifest before the judg-ment-seat of Christ; that each one may receive the things *done* in the body, according to what he hath done, whether *it be* good or bad.**

For Paul makes it his aim to be well-pleasing to Christ be-cause he is to be judged by Christ, and so are the hyper-critical Corinthians!

we must all Although there is no way of evading the force of this divine 'must' which applies to all men, 'all men do not have minds sufficiently exalted to remember every single moment that they must appear before the judgment-seat of Christ' (Calvin). Paul speaks of the one general judgment of all men by Christ, before whose tribunal even Christians must stand. 'It is impossible to identify a series of distinct and separate judgments' (G. E. Ladd, 'Eschatology', *The New Bible Dictionary*, p. 389). [Cf *Matt* 25.31–46; *John* 12.48; *Acts* 17.30, 31; *Rom* 2.16; 2 *Tim* 4.1; 2 *Pet* 3.7]

be made manifest 'We are at all times, manifest to God; *then* we shall be so to the assembled intelligent universe and to ourselves; for the judgment shall be not only in order to assign the everlasting portion to each, but to vindicate God's righteousness, so that it shall be manifest to all his creatures, and even to the sinner himself' (Fausset).

before the judgment-seat of Christ; 'The judgment-seat of God' [*Rom* 14.10] is also 'the judgment-seat of Christ', be-cause God has ordained that the world shall be judged by the One it condemned [*Acts* 17.31]. 'The Judge on this great occasion is to be not God, absolutely considered, but the God-man in his office as mediatorial King. All judgment is said to be, not inherently his, but *committed* to him by the Father. *John* 5.22, 27' (A. A. Hodge, *The Confession of Faith*, p. 390).

[68]

in order that each one may *receive as his due* **the things done by means of his body,** (Plummer) All men are to be judged, but not in the mass. For each man will be individually assessed so that 'there will be exact correspondence between action and requital' (Theodoret cited by Plummer).

according to what he hath done, That all men will be judged according to their works is the consistent teaching of the New Testament [e.g. *Matt* 16.27; *Rom* 2.6; *Rev* 22.12]. The same principle which seals the doom of the wicked will be used to determine the reward of the righteous. For though salvation is not by works [*Rom* 3.24], every believer's work will be tested, and whether he is rewarded or suffers loss (but not punishment) will depend on how he has built on the one foundation of grace which is Jesus Christ [1 *Cor* 3.10–15].

whether *it be* **good or bad.** 'The change to the neuter singular is significant. It seems to imply that, although persons will be judged one by one and not in groups, yet conduct in each case will be judged as a whole. In other words, it is character rather than separate acts that will be rewarded (in the case of believers) or punished (in the case of unbelievers) ... It is habitual action that will be judged. And this explains the aorist; it is what he did during his lifetime that is summed up and estimated as a total. Human tribunals deal with crime; they have punishments, but no rewards. The Divine tribunal has both' (Plummer). [*John* 5.29)

*V*11: **Knowing therefore the fear of the Lord, we persuade men, but we are made manifest unto God; and I hope that we are made manifest also in your consciences.**

The purity of Paul's motives in preaching the gospel is guaranteed by the awe which this forthcoming judgment inspires in him. He is prompted to persuade men by the supreme desire faithfully to discharge the Lord's commission, and not by any spirit of self-interest. In fact it is only as a man has this integrity towards God that his preaching can have any real appeal to men, for those who are not faithful to God are never genuine with men.

but we are made manifest unto God; Because Paul knows that God already has a perfect knowledge of his heart, he seeks to be as open before God now as he must be at Christ's judgment-seat [*v* 10].

and I hope that we are made manifest also in your consciences. 'Their consciences, rather than their intellects, on which they prided themselves: *conscience penetrates further than the judgment of the flesh*; conscience goes deeper than criticism (Calvin). Paul says "consciences" and not "conscience", because he appeals to the individual conscience of each of them: *the plural has greater weight* (Bengel)' (Plummer).

*V*12: **We are not again commending ourselves unto you, but** *speak* **as giving you occasion of glorying on our behalf, that ye may have wherewith to answer them that glory in appearance, and not in heart.**

In thus defending his ministry Paul is not again indulging in the self-praise with which he was charged by his cynical critics in Corinth [3.1]. But that it should have proved necessary for their father in Christ to supply them with the ammunition to repel these slanders was indeed a reproach to the Corinthians. 'Paul's opponents boasted of what was outward and incidental, personal knowledge of Jesus, connexion with the older apostles, Jewish descent and privilege, learning, eloquence, etc. By "heart" is meant the inward as contrasted with the outward, the essential as opposed to the incidental; so "spiritual reality" ' (Massie). [1 *Sam* 16.7]

*V*13: **For whether we are beside ourselves, it is unto God; or whether we are of sober mind, it is unto you.**

Like his Master before him, Paul was accused of religious dementia [*Mark* 3.21; *Acts* 26.24], but his 'fanaticism' was for God! Just as the Corinthians should be the last to deny the enlightening effect upon them of his lucid ministry of the gospel! The first part of the verse does not describe a state of religious ecstasy, for though Paul was no stranger to such experiences there is no reason to believe that the Corinthians ever saw him in this condition. On the contrary, he has to inform them of these *private* spiritual experiences [12.1; 1 *Cor* 14.18]. 'For God' and 'for you' are not in opposition, and do not exclude each other as though 'for God' meant 'for him and not for you', and 'for you' meant 'for you and not for God' (Lenski). *All* that Paul did and does is for God *and* for you!

*V*14: **For the love of Christ constraineth us; because we thus judge, that one died for all, therefore all died;**

It is the love of Christ for Paul which irresistibly impels him to serve God and his people in this way. This is the secret of stability in Christian service. The surpassing love of Christ for us must be reflected in our single-minded devotion to him [*Gal* 2.20]. This is how Paul defends his conduct before the Corinthians: 'Christ's love claims him in such a way that in relation to others he can no longer exist for himself – in contrast to his opponents, who boast to the Corinthians that they are religious and spiritual, that they are something in themselves' (H. Köster, *TDNT*, Vol. VII, pp. 883–4).

because we thus judge, 'lit., (as) "having judged thus"; implying a judgment formed at conversion, and ever since regarded as a settled truth' (Fausset).

[71]

that one died for all, therefore all died; The inescapable meaning of this statement is that the 'all' for whom Christ died are those who also died 'in the person of their representative' (F. F. Bruce). [cf *Rom* 5.12ff; 1 *Cor* 15.22] 'The nature of the atonement settles its extent. If it merely made salvation possible, it applied to all men. If it effectively secured salvation, it had reference only to the elect. As Dr Warfield says, "The things we have to choose between are an atonement of high value, or an atonement of wide extension. The two cannot go together". The work of Christ can be universalized only by evaporating its substance' (Loraine Boettner *The Reformed Doctrine of Predestination*, pp. 152–3).

*V*15: **and he died for all, that they that live should no longer live unto themselves, but unto him who for their sakes died and rose again.**

To die with Christ is 'to die to sin and to rise with him to the life of new obedience, to live not to ourselves but to him who died for us and rose again. The inference is inevitable that those for whom Christ died are those and those only who die to sin and live to righteousness. Now it is a plain fact that not all die to sin and live in newness of life. Hence we cannot say that all men distributively died with Christ. And neither can we say that Christ died for all men, for the simple reason that all for whom Christ died also died in Christ. If we cannot say that Christ died for all men, neither can we say that the atonement is universal – it is the death of Christ for men that specifically constitutes the atonement. The conclusion is apparent – the death of Christ in its specific character as atonement was for those and those only who are in due time the partakers of that new life of which Christ's resurrection is the pledge and pattern. This is another reminder that the death and resurrection of Christ are inseparable. Those for whom Christ died are those for whom he rose again and his heavenly

saving activity is of equal extent with his once-for-all redemp-
tive accomplishments' (John Murray, *Redemption Accomplished
and Applied,* pp. 70–1).

*V*16: **Wherefore we henceforth know no man after the
flesh: even though we have known Christ after the flesh,
yet now we know *him so* no more.**

'Wherefore' points to one consequence of the foregoing statement [v 15], another is advanced by the same word in the
following verse. 'After the flesh' here means '*the external* or
outward side of life, as it appears to the eye of an unregenerate
person' (Arndt-Gingrich). What Paul is saying is that since
his conversion he no longer estimates any man according to
worldly standards of judgment. For that which was natural
to the old mode of living is entirely unnatural to one who has
been raised to new life in Christ. But because the Judaizing
teachers are not thus constrained by the love of Christ, they
still judge 'after the flesh' and are influencing the Corinthians
to regard Paul in the same way. Paul knows this tendency
must be checked, for when Christians begin to look upon
others in a fleshly way, they are 'in the greatest danger of again
knowing Christ only in a fleshly way' (Lenski).

even though we have known Christ after the flesh, Paul
does not claim personal acquaintance with Jesus; he disowns
his former unworthy estimate of Christ as a blasphemer whose
death was merited and whose followers deserved the same
treatment [*Acts* 26.9–12]. But the judgment of Saul the unconverted Pharisee and that of Paul the believing Apostle
are poles apart.

yet now we know *him so* no more. It 'is not the figure of
Jesus who once wandered through the fields of Galilee, nor

is it the historical picture of the Nazarene, which forms the content of Paul's preaching; but it is the living Lord, who has been exalted out of his humiliation, and who as such is now the Lord of the Church ... Yet this does not say that Paul preached a different Jesus than the Jesus according to the flesh. Paul preached the same Christ, but Paul now proclaims a Jesus who died, and rose again, and who now sits at the right hand of God, the Father. The difference does not lie in the fact that the one picture is historical and human, whereas the other is super-historical and divine; but it lies in the fact that the history of redemption had progressed, that the Christ according to the flesh is now the Lord of the heavens' (Herman Ridderbos, *Paul and Jesus,* p. 69).

V17: **Wherefore if any man is in Christ, *he is* a new creature: the old things are passed away; behold, they are become new.**

Wherefore if any man is in Christ, there is a new creation: (ASV margin) What Paul has experienced is also true of every man who is in Christ. Because the Christian is in fact a new creation – 'a reborn microcosm belonging to the eschatological macrocosm' (P. E. Hughes) – he not only has a different standard of judgment from the man of the world, but is also the inhabitant of a totally new world. Hence the transformation effected by his union with Christ may not be restricted to his subjective renewal, for it includes his transfer into a world which has assumed a new aspect and complexion. This interpretation is required by the formula 'in Christ', which Paul nowhere uses in an exclusively individual sense: Christ 'is everywhere, where the formula in question occurs, the central dominating factor of a new order of affairs, in fact nothing less than the originator and representative of a new world-order' (Vos). [*Rev.* 21.4, 5]

the old things are passed away; behold, they are become new. 'Old opinions, views, plans, desires, principles and affections are passed away; new views of truth, new principles, new apprehensions of the destiny of man, and new feelings and purposes fill and govern the soul' (Hodge). [*Phil* 3.7]

*V*18: **But all things are of God, who reconciled us to himself through Christ, and gave unto us the ministry of reconciliation;**

But all things are of God, All these new things come from God. 'The new creation is no spontaneous development, and it is not man's own work on himself; Apostles do not claim to be the cause of it. It is wholly from God [*v* 5; 1.21, 2.14, 4.6; 1 *Cor* 8.6, 11.12; *Rom* 11.36]' (Plummer).

who reconciled us to himself through Christ, 'Reconciliation' in the New Testament sense 'is not something which *we accomplish* when we lay aside our enmity to God; it is something which *God accomplished* when in the death of Christ He put away everything that on His side meant estrangement, so that He might come and preach peace ... The serious thing which makes the Gospel necessary, and the putting away of which constitutes the Gospel, is God's condemnation of the world and its sin; it is God's wrath, "revealed from heaven against all ungodliness and unrighteousness of men" [*Rom* 1.16–18]. The putting away of this is "reconciliation": the preaching of *this* reconciliation is the preaching of the Gospel' (Denney).

and gave unto us the ministry of reconciliation; That a former persecutor of the church of God should have been entrusted with 'the ministry of reconciliation' never ceases to amaze Paul. But it is only because God has initiated and completed this great work of reconciliation that there is such a

[75]

service to perform. 'For unless we can preach a finished work of Christ in relation to sin, a reconciliation or peace which has been achieved independently of us at an infinite cost and to which we are called in a word or ministry of reconciliation, we have no real gospel for sinful men at all' (James Denney, *The Death of Christ,* p. 86).

*V*19: **to wit, that God was in Christ reconciling the world unto himself, not reckoning unto them their trespasses, and having committed unto us the word of reconciliation.**

that is, in Christ God was reconciling the world to himself, (RSV margin). The essence of the good news is that in Christ crucified God was reconciling the world unto himself. The term 'world' is neither to be arbitrarily limited to the elect, nor is it to be indiscriminately extended to each and every man, but it rather points to an 'eschatological' universalism. For as the whole creation was involved in the consequences of the Fall, so the cosmic restoration of all things is secured by Christ's cancellation of the curse of sin [*Rom* 8.19–21; *Col* 1.20].

not reckoning unto them their trespasses, and having committed unto us the word of reconciliation. 'The proof that God was reconciling the world to himself in Christ (i.e. in his death) is that he does not impute to men their trespasses, and that he has established the ministry of reconciliation. The forgiveness of sin and the institution of the ministry are clear evidence that God is propitious. Not to impute sin, is to forgive it. *Rom* 4, 5; 2 *Tim* 4, 16' (Hodge).

*V*20: **We are ambassadors therefore on behalf of Christ, as though God were entreating by us: we beseech *you* on behalf of Christ, be ye reconciled to God.**

So we are ambassadors for Christ, (RSV) As the representative of his sovereign, an ambassador delivers only what he has been commissioned to say, so that those who receive his message with contempt offend the king in whose name he speaks. Yet Christ's ambassadors are not quick to take offence on his behalf, and disregarding the obduracy of those to whom they are sent, they *beseech* (the word 'intimates an unusual submission' – Bengel) them to receive the proffered mercy of God. It is important to note that 'the interest of the statement is focused on the (material) authority of the message rather than the (formal) authority of an officer. Paul does not stress the latter even when defending his own apostleship, *Gal* 1.8; 1 *Thess* 2.7' (G. Bornkamm, *TDNT*, Vol. VI, p. 682).

God making his appeal through us. (RSV) 'The fact that "God is entreating by us" is a momentous one, and the declaration of it is analogous to the formula of the Hebrew Prophet, "Thus saith the Lord" ' (Plummer).

'We beseech on behalf of Christ: "Be reconciled to God!" ' (P. E. Hughes) This entreaty is not addressed to the Christians in Corinth, who are here reminded of the content of the apostle's constant appeal to the unconverted. 'The synergistic reasoning is fallacious that, since God tells men to be reconciled, men must have the ability to obey. The imperative is passive; it does not say: "Reconcile yourselves to God!" "Turn thou me, and I shall be turned!" *Jer* 31.18. Reconcile *thou* me, and I shall be reconciled! Every gospel imperative is full of the divine power of grace to effect what it demands. If it counted on even the least power in the sinner it would never secure the least effect. Jesus calls this the Father's drawing [*John* 6.44; 6.65; 12.32]' (Lenski).

*V*21: **Him who knew no sin he made *to be* sin on our behalf; that we might become the righteousness of God in him.**

[77]

In this tremendous sentence Paul explains what he means by the words, 'not reckoning unto them their trespasses' [v 19]. The non-imputation of sin rests on the fact that Christ our substitute was made sin on our behalf. And it is this objective *satisfaction* for sin that guarantees the reality of the reconciliation which the apostle beseeches men to receive.

Him who knew no sin 'That is, with a practical knowledge; with an intellectual he did, else he could not have reproved it. We know no more than we practise. Christ is said to "know no sin", because he did none' (Trapp). [*John* 8.46; *Heb* 4.15; 1 *Pet* 2.22; 1 *John* 3.5]

he made *to be* sin on our behalf; Only the One who knew no sin was free to bear its curse for others [*Gal* 3.13]. As the consequences of sin were charged to Christ's account, he became so closely identified with it that Paul even dares to say that God made him to be *sin*. Nevertheless this is a very different thing from saying that God made him a sinner. For though he exhausted the curse of sin, he was never personally defiled by it. 'While He was personally the object of the Father's everlasting love and complacency, He was officially guilty in our guilt. The paternal and the governmental on the part of God may easily be distinguished and viewed apart. He never was the object of the Father's loathing or aversion, even when forsaken. He never was, what the sinner inevitably is, abhorred, or abominable; because a distinction could always be made between the only begotten Son, the righteous Servant, and the sin-bearing Substitute' (G. Smeaton). [*Is* 53.4, 5]

that we might become the righteousness of God in him. The full meaning of our justification is disclosed in the amazing thought that we become 'the righteousness of God' by union with Christ [cf *Rom* 5.17, 18, 19]. 'We are made not only the beneficiaries of it; we are made the partakers of it and to such an extent that we are actually identified in terms of it. It is ours in the sense that our identity is defined in terms of it. Just as Christ became so identified with our sins that, though knowing no sin, he was made sin, so we being in ourselves utterly ungodly and therefore knowing no righteousness are so identified with Christ's righteousness that we are made the righteousness of God. In reality the concept is richer than that of imputation; it is not simply reckoned as ours, but it is reckoned to us and we are identified with it' (John Murray, *Collected Writings,* Vol. 2, p. 214). The early Christian writer of the Epistle to Diognetus also gave memorable expression to this truth in the rapturous words: 'O sweet exchange. O inscrutable operation. O unexpected blessings: that the lawlessness of many should be hidden in one righteous Person, and the righteousness of One should justify the lawless many' (cited by J. W. C. Wand, *A History of the Early Church,* pp. 61–2).

CHAPTER SIX

As a worker together with God, Paul entreats the Corinthians not to frustrate God's grace in the acceptable day of salvation [vv 1, 2]. In the discharge of his ministry he avoided all offence, proving his sincerity by patiently enduring all the trials which served to enrich others with the gospel [vv 3–10]. Paul speaks so freely because his heart is enlarged towards the Corinthians, and he urges them to enlarge their hearts towards him [vv 11–13]. They also must hold back from any intimate association with unbelievers since fellowship between righteousness and iniquity is impossible. Christians must shun all uncleanness because they are the temple of the living God [vv 14–18].

$V$1: **And working together *with him* we entreat also that ye receive not the grace of God in vain**

In the full consciousness that he is working together with God, Paul also appeals to the Corinthians, who have already received the message of reconciliation, that they do not receive this grace of God in vain. This means that there was a danger that the forthcoming judgment [5.10] would disclose a painful discrepancy between their practice and their profession [5.15]. They must see to it that they receive the grace of God *as grace*, and not as legalism or licence, or that day will find them barren of the righteousness which is the fruit of a living union with Christ.

*V*2: (for he saith,
        At an acceptable time I hearkened unto thee,
        And in a day of salvation did I succour thee:
behold, now is the acceptable time; behold, now is the
day of salvation):

This parenthetic appeal to Scripture is made to remind the
Corinthians that they have the inestimable privilege of living
in the promised season of grace [*Is* 49.8]. Here Paul takes the
answer that God gives to the prayer of his suffering Servant
(Christ) as assuring the salvation of all those for whom he is
the chosen Representative. Paul's own comment on the passage consists of an urgent summons to embrace the proffered
favour of God in the period appointed by God for its accept-
ance. He thereby lets the Corinthians know that the privilege
of living in such days of gospel opportunity also lays upon
them the solemn responsibility of seeing that they do not
receive the grace of God in vain [*v* 1].

*V*3: **giving no occasion of stumbling in anything, that
our ministration be not blamed;**

The connection is with verse 1, 'we entreat ... giving no
occasion of stumbling'. The consciousness that he is a worker
together with God leads the apostle to conduct himself in a
manner which is consistent with the ministry he has to exercise. 'Ministers give occasion of stumbling when by their own
faults they hinder the progress of the Gospel in those who
hear them. Paul claims that he is not of that company and
testifies to his careful concern not to stain his apostleship with
any taint of disgrace. For this is a trick of Satan – to seek for
a fault in ministers which will tend to bring the Gospel into
disrepute. For if he succeeds in bringing the ministry into contempt, all hope of progress is gone. Thus the man who wishes

2C.—6

to make himself useful in Christ's service must devote all his energies to maintaining the honour of his ministry' (Calvin).

V4: **but in everything commending ourselves, as ministers of God, in much patience, in afflictions, in necessities, in distresses, 5 in stripes, in imprisonments, in tumults, in labours, in watchings, in fastings;**

Paul is not like the false teachers who brandish wordy commendations of themselves [3.1], for his whole life is a constant validation of the message he proclaims. 'In much patience' is that quality of patient endurance which enables the apostle to triumph over trials of every kind. The nine afflictions listed fall into three groups.

in afflictions, in necessities, in distresses, The first 'triplet of trials' provides a climactic description of the general pressures to which he is subjected. 'In *afflictions* (crushings), many ways are open, but they are all difficult; in *necessities* (constraints), one way is open, though difficult; in *distresses* (straits), none is open' (Bengel).

in stripes, in imprisonments, in tumults, He turns next to particular hardships inflicted upon him by other men. His ministry was punctuated by brutal beatings which would have silenced a less determined spirit [11.23–25], frequently interrupted by imprisonments [11.23], and often abruptly halted by mob violence [*Acts* 13.50; 14.19; 16.19; 19.29].

in labours, in watchings, in fastings; Finally, he refers to the hardships he inflicted upon himself in the course of his work. In the cause of Christ he willingly submitted to 'wearing toil, sleepless nights, and hungry days' (Massie). [11.27]

*V*6: **in pureness, in knowledge, in long suffering, in kindness, in the Holy Spirit, in love unfeigned, 7 in the word of truth, in the power of God;**

Paul has been enabled to endure all these things in virtue of those spiritual graces that constitute the sphere or element in which his ministry moves.

in pureness, in knowledge, In the first pair of graces, Paul significantly couples purity of life and motive with the saving knowledge of the gospel, for both are always found together in all authentic ministry.

in long suffering, in kindness, The injuries inflicted upon Paul by the Corinthians had given him ample opportunity to exhibit his long suffering towards them and to repay their ingratitude with kindness [1 *Cor* 13.4; *Col* 3.12].

in the Holy Spirit, in love unfeigned, The holiness, of which the Holy Spirit himself is the author, displays itself in a love that is devoid of the least tincture of insincerity or hypocrisy [*Rom* 12.9; 1 *Pet* 1.22].

in the word of truth, in the power of God; Paul's proclamation of the word of truth was effective because he did not rely on persuasive words of wisdom to make it so, but trusted in the power of God [1 *Cor* 2.3ff]. He who is a stranger to the subjective power of the gospel in his own life cannot fittingly communicate its objective truth to others.

*V*7b: **by the armour of righteousness on the right hand and on the left. 8 by glory and dishonour, by evil report and good report;**

by the armour of righteousness on the right hand and on the left, The sword was held in the right hand, and the shield in the left [cf *Eph* 6.13–17]. 'The weapons by which he makes the "power of God" felt are characterized by a righteous temper, and they smite, or ward off smiting, in a righteous cause. They are not "fleshly weapons" [10.3, 4]. Paul's instruments of attack and defence, his sword and his shield, are righteous both as to means and as to end' (Massie).

by glory and dishonour, These opposing estimates of Paul's ministry nevertheless agree in recommending the devotion with which he prosecuted it. 'Some said, "He is beside himself", and others would have plucked out their eyes for his sake, yet both these extremely opposite attitudes were produced by the very same thing – the passionate earnestness with which he served Christ in the Gospel' (Denney).

by evil report and good report; Paul continues faithful to his calling whether slandered in his absence or flattered to his face. '*In proportion as a man has more or less of* glory *or* good report, *in the same proportion has he also more or less of either* disgrace *or* infamy *respectively*' (Bengel).

*V*8b: **as deceivers, and *yet* true; 9 as unknown, and *yet* well known; as dying, and behold, we live; as chastened, and not killed; 10 as sorrowful, yet always rejoicing; as poor, yet making many rich; as having nothing, and *yet* possessing all things.**

as deceivers, and *yet* true; In the first three couplets Paul has in view the dishonour which was heaped upon him by the evil report of his opponents in Corinth. In branding God's inspired apostle as a purveyor of deceit, these men declared themselves to be the true children of the father of lies, thus proving their own bondage to the arch-deceiver himself [*John* 8.44; 2 *John* 7].

as unknown, and *yet* well known; Paul's credentials may indeed be called in question by men, but he is confident that he is well known to God [2 *Tim* 2.19]. 'To be unknown to the world matters nothing; it is to be known of God as His own that is all-important' (P. E. Hughes).

as dying, and behold, we live; He is regarded by many as the doomed champion of a lost cause, but just when men are prepared to write him off as finished, all are surprised to find that he goes on living and serving his Lord.

as chastened, and not killed; Leaving these calumnies behind, Paul devotes the remaining four couplets to a paradoxical description of his actual condition. Here he thankfully acknowledges with the Psalmist, that though he is the subject of divine chastening (though *never* of divine wrath), God has not given him over to death [*Ps* 118. 17, 18].

as sorrowful, yet always rejoicing; Although constantly surrounded by every kind of grief, nothing could sever him from the source of his continual rejoicing. Thus it was from the cheerless gloom of a Roman gaol that he urged his fellow-believers in Philippi to follow his own example: 'Rejoice in the Lord always: again I will say, Rejoice' [*Phil* 4.4].

as poor, yet making many rich; That the apostle was not well endowed with worldly wealth was evident to all, yet it was given to him to make many rich through his preaching of 'the unsearchable riches of Christ' [*Eph* 3.8].

as having nothing, and *yet* possessing all things. 'It is no loss to have nothing and no gain to have everything in the way in which the world has and has not; but to have as Christians have is to have everything, no matter how little they have according to the world's way of having' (Lenski). [1 *Cor* 3.21ff].

*V*11: **Our mouth is open unto you, O Corinthians, our heart is enlarged.**

The emotions aroused in Paul by the complete lack of reserve with which he has spoken of his ministry here overflow in a sudden upsurge of feeling for his beloved converts at Corinth, to whom he addresses the tender appeal: 'O Corinthians' [cf *Gal* 3.1; *Phil* 4.15]. Since such openness of speech only flows from great enlargement of heart, they should no longer doubt the genuineness of his love for them. 'Love, like heat, expands' (Fausset).

*V*12: **Ye are not straitened in us, but ye are straitened in your own affections. 13 Now for a recompense in like kind (I speak as unto *my* children), be ye also enlarged.**

Paul here insists that there is no restraint or reserve in his love for them. 'The scanty room was not in him, but in the seat of their own affections, and it hampered *his* free admission to *their* hearts. Even now the feeling in Corinth towards him was not all that he could desire' (Waite). But if even as an apostle he cannot command their love, it is only natural that as their own father in the faith he should expect his love for them to be returned 'in the same way in exchange' (Arndt-Gingrich).

*V*14: **Be not unequally yoked with unbelievers: for what fellowship have righteousness and iniquity? or what communion hath light with darkness?**

The sudden transition from tender entreaty to stern admonition has led many to suppose that this passage [6.14–7.1] is a misplaced fragment from another letter, and in a number of modern commentaries the text is even re-arranged in accordance with this unproven and indeed unprovable hypothesis! In fact there is no evidence that any copy of the Epistle ever lacked these verses. Certainly the change in tone is abrupt, but the connection is clear enough. As Plummer rightly remarks, 'It is not incredible that in the middle of his appeal for *mutual* frankness and affection, and after his declaration that the cramping constraint is all on their side, he should dart off to one main cause of that constraint, viz. their compromising attitude towards anti-Christian influences.'

Be not unequally yoked with unbelievers: The allusion is to the law which forbade the uniting of animals of different species in the same yoke [*Deut* 22.10]. 'What a picture: a believer with his neck under the unbeliever's yoke! What business has he in such an unnatural, self-contradictory association? What is he, the believer, doing by helping to pull the plough or the wagon of the unbeliever's unbelief? That yoke breaks the necks of those who bear it. God has delivered us from it; can we possibly think of going back to that frightful yoke?' (Lenski). [cf *Matt* 11.28–30] Paul follows this command with five rhetorical questions that highlight the absolute incompatibility which exists between Christians and pagans.

for what fellowship have righteousness and iniquity? (literally: lawlessness) While it is true that in this world there are many points of contact between saints and sinners [1 *Cor* 5.10], it is self-evident that the opposing principles which characterize each class rule out any possibility of a partnership between them. For what fellowship has the *righteousness* of those who are distinguished by their habitual conformity to the law of God, with the *lawlessness* of those who are marked out by their unvarying opposition to it? [1 *John* 3.4, 9, 10].

or what communion hath light with darkness? Since nothing can be more incongruous than light and darkness, the attempt of 'Christians to remain Christians and retain their inward state as such, and yet to enter voluntarily into intimate fellowship with the world, is as impossible as to combine light and darkness, holiness and sin, happiness and misery' (Hodge).

V15: **And what concord hath Christ with Belial? or what portion hath a believer with an unbeliever?**

And what concord hath Christ with Beliar? (ASV margin) This question brings into view the personal rulers behind these qualities and powers. Only the most fundamental antagonism can exist between Christ, who is the personification of right-eousness, and Beliar (Satan), who is the personification of law-lessness. 'Christ hath no fellowship with the devil, therefore we ought to have no unnecessary communion with such who manifest themselves to be of their father the devil, by doing his works' (Matthew Poole).

or what portion hath a believer with an unbeliever? 'As subjects of their respective lords, what "portion" have they together? What the one has, the other has not: righteousness, pardon, spiritual light and life, peace, hope of salvation, a place in heaven. The portions of these two diverge at every point' (Lenski). Obviously, there can be no fellowship be-tween those whose respective destinies are so different. But the antithesis 'must not be interpreted as though it encouraged pharisaic concepts of contamination or invited to eremitic and monastic attempts at segregation from "the world"' (P. E. Hughes).

[88]

*V*16a: **And what agreement hath a temple of God with idols?**

What agreement hath God's sanctuary with idols?
(Plummer) This translation is preferable since Paul uses the word which refers to the temple as the very dwelling-place of God. The climax is reached in the final question, which provides the premiss for what follows [*vv* 16b–18]. For it exhibits the utter sinfulness of attempting to find a place for the images of false gods within the imageless sanctuary of God. 'By the introduction of idols the temple ceases to be a temple of God' (Plummer).

*V*16b: **for we are a temple of the living God; even as God said, I will dwell in them, and walk in them; and I will be their God, and they shall be my people.**

In boldly identifying 'the temple of the living God' (RSV) with the New Testament church (the emphatic 'we' = believers), Paul here condemns the carnal expectations which are fostered by a literalistic interpretation of Old Testament prophecy. 'There cannot be a surer canon of interpretation, than that *everything which affects the constitution and destiny of the New Testament Church has its clearest determination in New Testament Scripture*. This canon, with the grounds on which it is based, strikes at the root of many false conclusions drawn mainly from ancient prophecy, respecting the events of the latter days – conclusions which always implicitly, and sometimes even avowedly, give to the Old the ascendency over the New; and, on the principle which has its grand embodiment in Popery, would send the world back to the age of comparative darkness and imperfection for the type of its normal and perfected condition' (Patrick Fairbairn, *The Interpretation of Prophecy*, p. 158). [cf *Eph* 2.21; 1 *Pet* 2.5]

[89]

even as God said, I will dwell in them, and walk in them; and I will be their God, and they shall be my people. The distinctive thought of *Lev* 26.11–12 is that God will dwell *among* his people by means of the material sanctuary, whereas Paul's paraphrase is designed to bring out the fact that under the New Covenant he now dwells *in* them [cf *Eph* 2.22]. 'Paul assumes that the ancient promise fulfilled in outward and symbolic form in the ritual of the Tabernacle, is valid now; and assures believers of the inward and spiritual presence of God in themselves. For the entire ritual was an outward symbol of the spiritual realities of the better covenant (Beet) [*Ezek* 37.27].

*V*17: **Wherefore**
   Come ye out from among them, and be ye separate, saith the Lord,
      And touch no unclean thing;
      And I will receive you,

Wherefore The truth expressed in the foregoing quotation is now also applied in words which are freely drawn from Scripture [*vv* 17, 18].

Come ye out from among them ... And touch no unclean thing; God's warning to the returning exiles to leave everything that was unclean behind them in Babylon is here appropriately repeated to those so lately delivered from the idolatry of Corinth [*Is* 52.11].

And I will receive you, Such a separation is the necessary preparation for fellowship with God [*Ezek* 20.34]. 'The Christian life is thus seen to be no barren renunciation, for the believer is separated from the world for no less a purpose than that he may enjoy friendship with God in the blessed company of other faithful people' (Tasker).

*V*18: **And will be to you a Father,**
And ye shall be to me sons and daughters,
saith the Lord Almighty.

The final quotation, which combines 2 *Sam* 7.14 and *Is* 43.6, shows that if believers are corporately God's temple, individually they are members of God's family (so Murray Harris). Paul here adapts God's promise to David that his son would build him a house, in order to describe its spiritual fulfilment through David's greater Son [cf *John* 2.18–22]. Indeed Solomon's words at the dedication of the Temple indicate that he was well aware of its limitations [1 *Kings* 8.27; Acts 7.48]. 'It was only when the Christ, born of David's seed, dwelt in the hearts of those who accepted His sacrifice, and submitted themselves to the guidance of His Spirit, that God "became to them really as a Father, and they became His sons and daughters"' (R. V. G. Tasker, *The Old Testament in the New Testament*, p. 95). As the favoured recipients of such great promises, the Corinthians must therefore take care to shun the defilement which would debar them from their benefits [7.1].

CHAPTER SEVEN

After exhorting the Corinthians to purity of life, Paul again urges them to return his love, for he had neither wronged them nor lost confidence in them [vv 1–4]. On resuming the account of his movements, he recalls his anxiety as he awaited the return of Titus, and expresses his joy in their repentance [vv 5–7]. For though his severe letter had made them sorry, he did not now regret sending it, since their godly sorrow had produced such good effects [vv 8–12]. Above all, he rejoiced that the news brought by Titus had confirmed his trust in them [vv 13–16].

*V*1: **Having therefore these promises, beloved, let us cleanse ourselves from all defilements of flesh and spirit, perfecting holiness in the fear of God.**

As this verse concludes the paragraph begun at 6.14, the chapter division is particularly unfortunate here. In placing the emphasis on the word 'these', Paul underlines the privileges enjoyed by the Corinthians to enforce the obligations of obedience. 'Beloved' intensifies this appeal by conveying the warmth of his feeling for them [cf 12.19; *Rom* 12.19; 1 *Cor* 10.14; 15.58; *Phil* 2.12; 4.1]. It is not from any sense of mock humility that Paul includes himself in his exhortation, for even an apostle must strive to attain the goal of perfection [*Phil* 3.12–14]. The determinative, decisive act of cleansing is to be realized in the continual and continuing bringing of holiness to completion. Hence he speaks of 'perfecting holiness', not *perfected* holiness! 'The durative participle excludes sanctification that is attained by one act; moreover, *our* actions are here stated and not an action by which God totally sanctifies us in one instant' (Lenski). Thus all believers are required by God to cleanse themselves from everything that would defile either body ('flesh') or soul ('spirit'). But those who are unwilling to cleanse themselves from every *stain* of sin only show that they have not been cleansed from the *guilt* of sin. The unsanctified are the unjustified. 'In the fear of God' is 'the motive which is to determine our endeavours to purify ourselves. It is not regard to the good of others, nor our own happiness, but reverence for God. We are to be holy, because he is holy' (Hodge). (1 *Pet* 1.14–17]

*V*2: **Open your hearts to us: we wronged no man, we corrupted no man, we took advantage of no man.**

Paul now returns to the appeal of 6.11–13. Since the Corinthians occupy so large a place in his affections, surely they can return his love by making room for him in their hearts! That he had harmed no one was made manifest in their consciences [5.11], and therefore he contents himself with a flat denial of the hollow charges which had been brought against him. 'Modestly he leaves them to supply the *positive* good which he had done; suffering all things himself that they might be benefited [*vv* 9, 12; 12.13]' (Fausset).

*V*3: **I say it not to condemn *you*: for I have said before, that ye are in our hearts to die together and live together.**
In thus protesting his innocence, the apostle has no desire to condemn those whom he loves so completely that not even the final crisis of death, much less the vicissitudes of life, can ever erase their image from his heart [cf 3.2; 6.11]. Paul may

put 'death' first because his recent experiences had made it a more likely prospect than life [1.8; 11.23].

V4: Great is my boldness of speech toward you, great is my glorying on your behalf: I am filled with comfort, I overflow with joy in all our affliction.

So far from wishing to condemn the Corinthians, Paul has every confidence in them and glories greatly on their behalf. In speaking here of '*the* comfort' and '*the* joy' (translating the article) with which he is filled to overflowing, he evidently refers to the effect produced by the news of their repentance which Titus had brought to him.

V5: For even when we were come into Macedonia our flesh had no relief, but we were afflicted on every side; without were fightings, within were fears.

Having concluded his great 'digression' on the glory of the ministry entrusted to him by God, Paul now returns to the point at which he broke off the account of his movements in 2.13. There, he says, 'I had no relief for my *spirit*'; here, 'our flesh had no relief'. This virtually synonymous usage shows that Paul's intense anxiety of spirit as he awaited the coming of Titus also affected his flesh, for the body is the vehicle through which the experience of the spirit finds its expression (so P. E. Hughes).

but *we were* afflicted on every side; without *were* fightings, within *were* fears. The situation is sketched with only three bold strokes, for Paul has no wish to dwell upon past sorrows now. Nevertheless, it is enough to let the Corinthians see something of the severity of his sufferings. For he was not only besieged by those outward troubles which were the usual accompaniment to his ministry, but he was also gripped by inward fears concerning 'the effects of his letter and of the mission of Titus' (Massie).

*V*6: **Nevertheless he that comforteth the lowly, *even* God, comforted us by the coming of Titus;**

But God, who comforts the downcast, (RSV) The right idea is not conveyed by the word 'lowly'. Paul was depressed and downcast by adverse circumstances. But the 'God of all comfort' [1.3] comforted his much tried servant by the arrival of Titus with the good news from Corinth [*Is* 49.13]. 'From this we may gather the most profitable lesson that the more we are afflicted, the greater is the comfort that God has prepared for us. And so this description of God contains a wonderful promise that it is specially God's concern to comfort the miserable and those bowed down to the dust' (Calvin).

*V*7: **and not by his coming only, but also by the comfort wherewith he was comforted in you, while he told us your longing, your mourning, your zeal for me; so that I rejoiced yet more.**

Determined to savour the word to the full, Paul says that he was not only comforted by the coming of Titus, but also by the comfort Titus had received from the Corinthians. The fact that Titus also needed comforting tells us something of the trepidation he felt as he undertook his difficult mission to Corinth. The comfort dispensed was threefold: 'your longing' refers to the Corinthians' longing to see Paul again and to reassure him of their affection; 'your mourning' to their sorrow for having caused him so much pain; 'your zeal for me' to their ardour in defending him and disciplining the offender [*vv* 11, 12]. Thus Paul's joy in meeting Titus was greatly increased when he learned how the Corinthians now regarded their apostle.

*V*8: **For though I made you sorry with my epistle, I do not regret it: though I did regret *it* (for I see that that epistle made you sorry, though but for a season), 9 I now rejoice, not that ye were made sorry, but that ye were made sorry unto repentance; for ye were made sorry after a godly sort, that ye might suffer loss by us in nothing.**

For though I made you sorry with my epistle, I do not regret it: though I did regret *it* The Corinthian revolt had forced Paul to send them a letter he would have preferred not to write, because he knew it would cause them pain (see Introduction and comment on 2.3, 4). But though he cannot now regret the happy consequences of sending this 'severe' letter, he was filled with misgivings after its despatch as he wondered how they would receive it. 'Paul's admission may serve as a great comfort to us. Neither revelation nor inspiration lifted the apostles above their poor "flesh" or human nature (here mentioned twice: 7.1, 5) which asserted itself in hours of weakness and depression in the form of even doubts and regrets' (Lenski).

(for I see that that epistle made you sorry, though but for a season), 'Gr. for an hour. In sin, the pleasure passeth, the sorrow remaineth; but in repentance, the sorrow passeth, the pleasure abideth for ever. God soon poureth the oil of gladness into broken hearts' (Trapp).

I now rejoice, not that ye were made sorry; but that ye were made sorry unto repentance; Since it gave their spiritual father no pleasure to cause the Corinthians pain, it was only the final result of his letter which brought Paul joy. His regret (*metamelomai*) gave way to rejoicing only when he learned that their sorrow had led to their repentance (*meta-*

noia). These words differ etymologically in that the former 'lays stress on the affliction or pain that is experienced on the contemplation of our former folly'; while the latter 'points primarily to the change of mind, issuing in amendment, which afterthought brings to us' ('New Testament Terms Descriptive of the Great Change': *Selected Shorter Writings of Benjamin B. Warfield,* Vol. I, p. 267).

for ye were made sorry after a godly sort, literally, 'according to God'. For when they saw their sin in the light of God's Word, they were made sorry 'in a manner agreeable to the mind and will of God; so that God approved of their sorrow. He saw that it arose from right views of their past conduct' (Hodge).

that ye might suffer loss by us in nothing. 'Those who have not experienced true repentance might conceive of it as a great loss; it is always the very opposite, the greatest spiritual gain. The grief of repentance is never loss in any way; not to experience this grief, that is loss indeed' (Lenski). (cf 'the sorrow of the world', *v* 10)

*V*10: **For godly sorrow worketh repentance unto salvation,** *a repentance* **which bringeth no regret: but the sorrow of the world worketh death.**

Here Paul carries over the idea of regretting and not-regretting from *v* 8. Such godly sorrow, a right regret for sin, is the essential preliminary to an 'unregrettable repentance', that gracious change of mind which always leads to salvation. Thus *metanoia* (repentance) 'does not properly signify the sorrow for having done amiss, but something that is nobler than it, but brought in at the gate of sorrow' (Jeremy Taylor, *On the Doctrine and Practice of Repentance,* cited by Trench).

but the sorrow of the world worketh death. Those who mourn over their sin turn from it and are saved; those who merely experience remorse over the bitter fruit of sin give way to despair and are lost [e.g. Judas Iscariot, *Matt* 27.3; Esau, *Heb* 12.17].

*V*11 : **For behold, this selfsame thing, that ye were made sorry after a godly sort, what earnest care it wrought in you, yea what clearing of yourselves, yea what indignation, yea what fear, yea what longing, yea what zeal, yea what avenging! In everything ye approved yourselves to be pure in the matter.**

For behold, this selfsame thing, that ye were made sorry after a godly sort, Behold this blessed result and admire what was wrought in you by the grace of God, for you are yourselves an example of the right kind of sorrow and its fruits!

what earnest care ... yea what avenging! Paul's delight in their repentance is expressed in seven particulars. 1. **earnest care** refers to the Corinthians' 'zealous concern' for the apostle, 'the concern to make restitution which results from true repentance ... It is obvious that this *earnestness* is a fruit of the Spirit which the Spirit brings forth through the apostle and his work in the church. Hence *earnestness* denotes a new attitude on the part of the Corinthians' (G. Harder, *TDNT*, Vol. VII, p. 566). 2. **clearing of yourselves** or 'self-vindication' describes their eagerness to show that they did not condone the offence. 3. **indignation.** This was directed against the one who had taken the lead in defying Paul and at themselves for having listened to him [2.5]. 4. **fear.** What they feared was not so much the apostle's rod as God's judgments. This is a fear which true repentance always awakens! 5. **longing** points to their yearning for the renewed favour and return of

Paul. 6. **zeal** relates to their ardour in defending the apostle against his accusers. 7. **avenging**. Finally, the punishment inflicted upon the offender attested the reality of their repentance [*v* 12; 2.6].

In everything ye approved yourselves to be pure in the matter. 'The matter' vaguely refers to what is best forgotten now that the church, through the action taken by the majority of its members, had shown itself to be free of blame in connection with the sin, which at first it appeared to condone.

V12: So although I wrote unto you, *I wrote* not for his cause that did the wrong, nor for his cause that suffered the wrong, but that your earnest care for us might be made manifest unto you in the sight of God.

Clearly, Paul does not mean that he had no concern for the offender (see comment on 2.5), or the one who had suffered the wrong (probably Paul himself), but that this was not the *primary* purpose in writing to them. Here Paul exhibits a common Hebrew mode of thought, in which one of two alternatives is negatived 'without meaning that it is negatived absolutely, but only in comparison with the other alternative, which is much more important. "I will have mercy, and not sacrifice" [*Hos* 6.6] does not prohibit sacrifice; it affirms that mercy is much the better of the two. Cf *Mark* 9.37; *Luke* 10.20, 14.12, 23.28' (Plummer).

but that your earnest care for us might be made manifest unto you in the sight of God. By putting to the proof their full obedience, Paul aroused their dormant love and loyalty so that in the presence of God they might become aware of how much he meant to them. The issue was not at all a question of personal pique on his part; it involved nothing less than their own future as Christians. For how could they continue in fellowship with Christ while they deliberately remained in a state of alienation from his chosen apostle?

*V*13: **Therefore we have been comforted: and in our comfort we joyed the more exceedingly for the joy of Titus, because his spirit hath been refreshed by you all.**

Therefore we have been comforted: This rounds off the thought of verse 12. The perfect tense indicates that Paul has been and remains comforted by the report Titus brought back from Corinth [*v* 6]. The second part of the verse introduces a new thought which is marked in many modern versions by a new paragraph [cf RSV, NEB, NIV]. The apostle's joy was augmented by the joyfulness of Titus at the success of a mission that was fraught with the greatest difficulties. But the Corinthians' warm welcome and ready obedience had brought a refreshment to his spirit that was still with him (perfect tense again).

*V*14: **For if in anything I have gloried to him on your behalf, I was not put to shame; but as we spoke all things to you in truth, so our glorying also which I made before Titus was found to be truth.**

Although Paul did not minimize the gravity of the crisis, he believed that at heart the Corinthians were loyal and true, and he had assured Titus that his mission would be crowned with success. Happily, Paul's confidence in them was justified by the event and so he was not put to shame. This negative has the affirmative meaning: 'Your response more than confirmed my words to Titus' (Lenski).

but as we spake all things to you in truth, so our glorying also which I made before Titus was found to be truth. ' "My words *about* you have proved as true as my words *to* you". A delicate hint that they should not have so readily accepted accusations against his genuineness [1.12–14] when he was all the while expressing confidence in them' (Massie).

*V*15: **And his affection is more abundantly toward you, while he remembereth the obedience of you all, how with fear and trembling ye received him.**

Titus' affection for the Corinthians is intensified as he recalls their willingness to obey the demands he had to make, and their 'nervous and trembling anxiety to do right' (Lightfoot on *Phil* 2.12). 'This passage teaches how ministers of Christ should be rightly received. It is not sumptuous banquets or splendid apparel or courteous and honourable salutations or the applause of crowds that give pleasure to a faithful and upright pastor: he has his sufficient joy when the doctrine of salvation is reverently received from his lips, when he can exercise the authority that belongs to him for the upbuilding of the Church, when the people submit themselves to his direction so as to be ruled by Christ through his ministry' (Calvin).

*V*16: **I rejoice that in everything I am of good courage concerning you.**

'This expression of generous confidence is both a natural conclusion to the present subject and a preparation for the frank exhortation on money matters in ch 8. It was only after the return to mutual confidence that such matters could be approached' (Massie).

CHAPTER EIGHT

*Paul now appeals to the Corinthians to finish the collection for the
relief of the saints at Jerusalem, and exhorts them to follow the
generous example set by the poor churches of Macedonia [vv 1–6].
As they abounded in every other grace, they should also abound in
the grace of giving. In thus calling their attention to the generosity
of others Paul issues no commands, for the supreme example of
Christ's self-giving should be enough to constrain their ready response. Each must decide how much he ought to give, so that his
abundance might help to supply the needs of others [vv 7–15].
Paul informs them that to avoid any occasion of blame, Titus and
two approved assistants will help them to complete the fund [vv
16–24].*

*V*1: **Moreover; brethren, we make known to you the
grace of God which hath been given in the churches of
Macedonia;**

Now we make known to you, brethen, This serves to in-
troduce a topic that deserves their close attention [cf 1 *Cor*
12.3; 15.1; *Gal* 1.11]. It concerns 'the collection' [1 *Cor* 16.1],
a collection 'which was not so much for "the *poor* in Jerusalem'
as for "the poor in *Jerusalem*" ' (K. L. Schmidt quoted by P.
E. Hughes). For it was by this means that Paul hoped to give
practical expression to that spiritual unity which both Jew
and Gentile now enjoyed in Christ [*Eph* 2.12–18].

the grace of God which hath been given in the churches of Macedonia; That Paul is able to devote two chapters of this Epistle to the subject of Christian giving without even mentioning the word 'money' is not only something of a *tour de force*, but it also serves to ennoble that which even Christians are apt to consider in a very materialistic manner (Denney). Here, for example, he cites the generosity of the Macedonian churches (which would include those at Philippi, Thessalonica, and Berœa) as an evidence of the grace of God that was still at work in their midst. 'Thus, while holding up human excellence as an example, he shuts out beforehand all human merit' (Beet). [*Eph* 2.10]

V2: **how that in much proof of affliction the abundance of their joy and their deep poverty abounded unto the riches of their liberality.**

(namely) **that in a great test of affliction the excess of their joy and their down-to-depth poverty exceeded in the riches of their single-mindedness.** (Lenski) Macedonia had been reduced to a state of grinding poverty by the crippling taxes of Rome, and in the case of these Christian communities this condition was made worse by persecution. And though affliction filled them with abounding joy, it reduced them to such dire straits that bounty seemed impossible. 'Yet these two opposites working in combination like an alkali and an acid, brought about an overflowing result which is called "the riches of their single-mindedness". Single-mindedness is that state of heart in which a man does not regard his own slender means nor any selfish consideration, but has his eye fixed exclusively upon his brother's needs. The Apostle says not that the contribution, but that the single-mindedness was rich, because it was *this* that he wished to awaken in the Corinthians. Should it operate upon Corinthian wealth

instead of Macedonian poverty, the harvest would be plentiful'
(Waite).

*V*3: **For according to their power, I bear witness, yea
and beyond their power,** *they gave* **of their own accord,
4 beseeching us with much entreaty in regard of this
grace and the fellowship in the ministering to the saints:
5 and** *this*, **not as we had hoped, but first they gave their
own selves to the Lord, and to us through the will of
God.**

The single occurrence of the verb 'gave' in verse 5 governs
the whole of this elaborate statement, which furnishes further
particulars of the liberality of the Macedonians.

1. Their help was on a scale quite beyond their slender resources. 'Despite their deep poverty they insisted on giving
far more than anyone could even think they could give. They
made a joy of robbing themselves' (Lenski).

2. It was rendered so willingly that they pleaded for the
'favour' (lit. 'grace') of being allowed to 'participate' (lit.
'fellowship') in ministering to the saints. 'They begged the
apostle to help them to an opportunity of acting upon the
generous desire which God had implanted within them, and
so of enjoying the sense of fellowship which "giving and receiving" [*Phil* 4.15] created' (Massie).

3. The secret of their unexpected generosity lay in their unreserved commitment to the Lord and his apostle. Theirs was
no slight contribution, for their gift was not of money merely,
'but of themselves, first and foremost, to the Lord, who gave
himself for them [*Gal* 1.4; 2.20], and also to the apostle, as
the minister, through whom Christ's self-sacrifice had been
made known to them, and through whom the work of love
for the saints was proceeding' (Waite).

*V*6: **Insomuch that we exhorted Titus, that as he had made a beginning before, so he would also complete in you this grace also.**

'This grace' refers to the collection (cf RSV: 'this gracious work'). It appears that Titus began the task of organizing the collection in Corinth on a former visit, probably before 1 Corinthians was written. P. E. Hughes suggests that he may have been the bearer of the 'previous' letter mentioned in 1 *Cor* 5.9. Happily, uncertainty on this point does not affect the general sense of the verse, which is well summarized by Fausset: 'As we saw the Macedonians' alacrity in giving, we could not but exhort Titus that, as we collected in Macedonia, so he in Corinth should complete the collection which he had already begun there, lest ye of wealthy Corinth should be outdone in liberality by the poor Macedonians'.

*V*7: **But as ye abound in everything, *in* faith, and utterance, and knowledge, and *in* all earnestness, and *in* your love to us, *see* that ye abound in this grace also.**

As Paul rejoiced that in everything the Corinthians were enriched in Christ [1 *Cor* 1.5], so he desires that they also might abound in the grace of giving. For if they failed 'in this respect, it would falsify his boast that they abound *in everything*. A gentler and more urbane method of incitement to generosity it would be difficult to imagine!' (P. E. Hughes).

*V*8: **I speak not by way of commandment, but as proving through the earnestness of others the sincerity also of your love.**

Because true liberality is the spontaneous expression of love, Paul refuses to command their charity. Instead he seeks to prove the genuineness of their love by means of the zeal of those in Macedonia. For as Hodge pertinently remarks, 'The real test of the genuineness of any inward affection is not so much the character of the feeling as it reveals itself in our consciousness, as the course of action to which it leads. Many persons, if they judged themselves by their feelings, would regard themselves as truly compassionate; but a judgment founded on their acts would lead to the opposite conclusion.'

*V*9: **For ye know the grace of our Lord Jesus Christ, that, though he was rich, yet for your sakes he became poor, that ye through his poverty might become rich.**

For ye know There is no need to command the Corinthians, for they *know* the grand motive to Christian charity. Paul expects their participation in this gracious work as the natural consequence of their experimental knowledge of the grace of Christ.

the grace of our Lord Jesus Christ, The glory of the Giver exhibits the greatness of the grace. It is the grace which comes to them through the infinite condescension of the One who is the *Lord* to whom they owe unqualified obedience, the *Saviour* to whom they owe their salvation, and the *Mediator* through whom they are reconciled to God.

that, though he was rich, 'i.e. though He shared His Father's glory before the world was created (see *John* 17.5), nevertheless He temporarily laid aside this glory in order to "be found in fashion as a man". He did not lay aside His divinity; for there is no doctrine of *kenōsis*, or emptying of His Godhead, to be found here any more than in *Phil* 2.7' (Tasker).

yet for your sakes 'Believers are to consider that Christ impoverished himself *for them* in order that they might be enriched in an immeasurably higher sense than that of worldly riches, and in gratitude, they are to follow his example on a humbler level, by doing an incomparably slighter thing, sacrificing a portion of their worldly substance to supply the natural needs of those who are Christ's' (Waite).

he became poor, The moment when 'he *became* poor' is marked by the aorist tense. It has been thought that this self-impoverishment carries an allusion to the poverty of the Lord's earthly life [*Matt* 8.20]; 'but the *primary* reference cannot be to this, for the "poverty" of Jesus Christ *by* which we are "made rich" is not the mere hardship and penury of his outward lot, but the state which he assumed in becoming man' (Bernard).

that ye through his poverty might become rich. 'Rich in "redemption through his blood, the forgiveness of sins", rich in "peace with God through our Lord Jesus Christ", rich in "newness of life", in objects to live for and motives to live by; rich in mastery over ourselves, the world, and the wicked one, in joy unspeakable and full of glory: "all things are ours, and we are Christ's, and Christ is God's" [1 *Cor* 3.22, 23]' (Brown).

*V*10: **And herein I give *my* judgment: for this is expedient for you, who were the first to make a beginning a year ago, not only to do, but also to will.**

And herewith I give my opinion; what I ask is for your advantage, since you took the lead in the matter as far back as last year not only in the doing but even in the willing. (Menzies) If Paul does not command [*v* 8], he leaves the Corinthians in no doubt of his opinion on the matter. For they had anticipated the Macedonians not only in resolving to make a collection, but also in their eagerness to contribute to it. 'Having thus been beforehand with them it would be to your disadvantage to leave your work half done, seeing that the mere mention of your purpose, ch 9.2, roused them to such self-denying liberality' (Hodge).

V11: **But now complete the doing also; that as *there was* the readiness to will, so *there may be* the completion also out of your ability.**

The Corinthians' initial enthusiasm for the collection must be matched by their determination to bring it to completion. For it would be a sad thing if 'those who were foremost in willing should be hindermost in performing; they must bring their performance into line with their willingness' (Plummer). Paul does not suggest that they should follow the example of the Macedonians by giving beyond their ability [*v* 3], but he looks for a contribution according to the measure of their ability [cf I *Cor* 16.2].

V12: **For if the readiness is there, *it is* acceptable according as *a man* hath, not according as *he* hath not.**

God measures the acceptability of the gift in the light of what a man has and the readiness with which it is given. 'For willingness to give is not judged by what you do not have, or, in other words, God never requires that you should contribute more than your resources allow. In this way none is left with any excuse since rich men owe God a large tribute and poor men have no reason to be ashamed if what they give is small' (Calvin). [cf *Mark* 12.41ff]

V13: **For *I say* not *this* that others may be eased *and* ye distressed; 14 but by equality: your abundance *being a supply* at this present time for their want, that their**

abundance also may become *a supply* for your want; that there may be equality:

It is not Paul's object to enrich others by impoverishing the Corinthians. He seeks an equality whereby their present wealth may supply the want of the saints in Jerusalem. Should this situation be reversed at some future date, then it would be for Jerusalem to send relief to them. He is not advocating an equality of goods, but speaks of an equal relief from the burden of want. The Scriptures 'avoid, on the one hand, the injustice and destructive evils of agrarian communism, by recognizing the right of property and making all almsgiving optional; and on the other, the heartless disregard of the poor by inculcating the universal brotherhood of believers, and the consequent duty of each to contribute of his abundance to relieve the necessities of the poor. At the same time they inculcate on the poor the duty of self-support to the extent of their ability' (Hodge). [2 *Thess* 3.10]

*V*15: **as it is written, He that *gathered* much had nothing over; and he that *gathered* little had no lack.**

Paul finds an illustration of the principle of equality in *Exod* 16.18. In the wilderness God saw to it that all the Israelites received the same measure of manna, whether they could gather much or little. 'The same equality is now to be established voluntarily in the Christian world. He who in the first instance has received (relatively) much, is not finally to "have more" than others' (G. Delling, *TDNT*, Vol. VI, p. 266).

*V*16: **But thanks be to God, who putteth the same earnest care for you into the heart of Titus.**

As Titus is to lead the delegation entrusted with the responsibility of collecting the Corinthians' gift for the saints in

Jerusalem, Paul thanks God for constantly giving Titus the same zeal for their welfare as he has himself. They should realize that this earnest care is in *their* interest, for they would only rob themselves of much spiritual enrichment if they failed to make a worthy contribution to the relief-fund.

*V*17: **For he accepted indeed our exhortation: but being himself very earnest, he went forth unto you of his own accord.**

When Paul urged Titus to undertake this task, his concern for the Corinthians was such that no persuasion was necessary. He was coming to them of his own accord. 'It was important for his work in Corinth that the Corinthians should know this. It was the best recommendation which Paul could send along with Titus' (Lenski).

went forth 'We should say, *he is going* forth; but the ancients put the *past* tense in letter-writing, as the things will have been past by the time that the correspondent receives the letter' (Fausset).

*V*18: **And we have sent together with him the brother whose praise in the gospel *is spread* through all the churches; 19 and not only so, but who was also appointed by the churches to travel with us in *the matter of* this grace, which is ministered by us to the glory of the Lord, and *to show* our readiness:**

Since Paul does not name the two brethren [*vv* 18, 22] who are to accompany Titus to Corinth, the attempt to identify them is quite pointless. What he is at pains to point out is that they are both tried and trusted men who have been officially appointed to perform this service by the churches [*v* 23].

Moreover, the appointment proves that Paul has no personal axe to grind in forwarding this gracious work. He seeks neither gain nor glory for himself, for his very eagerness to advance such a work of grace serves to manifest the glory of the Lord to whom he is devoted. It seems likely that this particular brother was renowned for his preaching of the gospel, though the reference may be to service of a more general nature.

*V*20: **avoiding this, that any man should blame us in** *the matter of* **this bounty which is ministered by us:**

The collection is organized by Paul, but the money will be collected by Titus and the two messengers who have been appointed by the churches for this purpose. This precaution is necessary to avoid giving anyone an opportunity to accuse the apostle of misappropriating any part of the fund [cf 12.17, 18]. He encourages the Corinthians to give generously by letting them know that he thinks of their contribution in terms of 'this lavish gift' (Arndt-Gingrich).

*V*21: **for we take thought for things honourable, not only in the sight of the Lord, but also in the sight of men.**

'This gives the reason for the precaution just mentioned. It was not enough for the apostle to do right, he recognized the importance of appearing right. It is a foolish pride which leads to a disregard of public opinion. We are bound to act in such a way that not only God, who sees the heart and knows all things, may approve our conduct, but also so that men may be constrained to recognize our integrity. It is a general principle regulating his whole life which the apostle here announces' (Hodge). [*Prov* 3.4 LXX; *Rom* 12.17]

*V*22: **And we have sent with them our brother, whom we have many times proved earnest in many things, but now much more earnest, by reason of the great confidence which *he hath* in you.**

Paul commends the second brother to the Corinthians on the double ground that his earnestness in *many* things has been proved on *many* previous occasions, and that he is now *much* more earnest through the *great* confidence which he has in them (after having heard the good report of Titus). The italicized words show how in the original Paul adds force to this commendation by using the same word four times.

*V*23: **Whether *any inquire* about Titus, *he is* my partner and *my* fellow-worker to you-ward; or our brethren, *they are* the messengers of the churches, *they are* the glory of Christ.**

'Paul extols the three in the highest terms before he sends them off; if anybody in Corinth wishes to know what they are, he is proud to tell. Titus is his partner in the apostolic calling, and has shared his work among them; the other brethren are deputies (apostles) of Churches, a glory of Christ' (Denney). Therefore let the Corinthians receive these duly authorized representatives in a way which befits those whose calling and character are a credit to Christ.

*V*24: **Show ye therefore unto them in the face of the churches the proof of your love, and of our glorying on your behalf.**

The chapter concludes 'with an exhortation to their liberality, backed with a heap of arguments. 1. It would be an evidence of their love to God, to their afflicted brethren, and to the apostle. 2. It would be a proof of it to those messengers of the churches, and to the churches whose messengers they were. 3. It would evidence that the apostle had not, to Titus and others, boasted on their behalf in vain' (Poole).

CHAPTER NINE

Although aware of the Corinthians' good intentions, Paul had sent the brethren to complete the collection, so that if any Macedonians accompanied him to Corinth he would not be put to shame by finding them unprepared [vv 1–4]. Such preparation was necessary to show that their contribution was freely given and not unwillingly extracted [v 5]. He encourages them to give bountifully and cheerfully, as the best way of increasing their graces and their means of doing good [vv 6–11]. This ministry to the saints redounds in thanksgiving to God, promotes the mutual love of believers, and exhibits their graces. Hence the apostle thanks God for the priceless boon of Christ, through whom this rich bounty of grace is produced [vv 12–15].

$V$1: **For as touching the ministering to the saints, it is superfluous for me to write to you:**

Since the word 'for' indicates a continuation of the same subject, the unfortunate chapter division should be ignored. Paul has been speaking in ch 8 of the need for promptness in making the collection, a promptness which will be a public proof of love [8.24]. 'As to the service itself, the ministering to the saints, about that he need write nothing; they have been inclined for that for some time back: it is their very inclination that leads him to send on the brethren' (Massie). [v 3]

*V*2: **for I know your readiness, of which I glory on your behalf to them of Macedonia, that Achaia hath been prepared for a year past; and your zeal hath stirred up very many of them.**

Paul's boasting concerns the readiness with which the Corinthians responded when the matter of the collection was first brought before them. They 'took it up eagerly, and were prepared to contribute at once and actually began [8.10] to contribute. Even the liberality of the Macedonians, for which Paul is so thankful to God, was in great part a result of the example thus nobly set by the Corinthians. All this proves that it is needless for him to write to them *about the collection*. But it does not prevent him from telling them of the liberality of the Macedonians, that the example of those whom their own liberal purpose had aroused might prompt them to complete at once the work they had been the first to begin. Thus example acts and re-acts' (Beet).

*V*3: **But I have sent the brethren, that our glorying on your behalf may not be made void in this respect; that, even as I said, ye may be prepared:**

But I am sending the brethren, lest the boast I have made of you should be proved an empty one in this particular, that you might be prepared, as I said you were. (Menzies) Paul is confident that his boasting on the Corinthians' behalf will be found true in every respect [8.7], except perhaps in this one particular. Of their readiness to will [8.11] he has no doubt, but if this is not matched by a similar alacrity in giving he is afraid that the preparations for the collection will be incomplete when he arrives in Corinth with the envoys from Macedonia. It is to avoid this embarrassment that he is sending Titus and his colleagues in advance so that his confidence in the Corinthians may be fully justified by the event.

V4: lest by any means, if there come with me any of Macedonia and find you unprepared, we (that we say not, ye) should be put to shame in this confidence.

lest if some Macedonians come with me and find that you are not ready, we be humiliated – to say nothing of you – for being so confident. (RSV) Paul is warning the Corinthians that when he comes to Corinth he will probably be accompanied by some Macedonians, the representatives of those whose zeal was stimulated by his account of their own enthusiasm for the collection. Let them imagine the disgrace it would be for him, to say nothing of themselves, if this visit found them still unprepared.

V5: I thought it necessary therefore to entreat the brethren, that they would go before unto you, and make up beforehand your aforepromised bounty, that the same might be ready as a matter of bounty, and not of extortion.

and not of covetousness. (ASV margin) To avoid this disgrace Paul thought it necessary to entreat Titus and his two assistants to 'come beforehand to you and set in order beforehand your blessing, which has been promised beforehand' (Waite). The emphatic repetition makes it impossible for the Corinthians to mistake Paul's meaning. The collection they had promised so long *before* must be completed *before* his arrival in Corinth! And since this fund is intended to minister a blessing to its recipients, let them give generously to it and not in such a manner as would betray a grudging or covetous spirit. 'Love blesses, whereas covetousness takes advantage of the brother by a close scrutiny of the gift, which becomes thereby a gift of covetousness' (G. Delling, *TDNT*, Vol. VI, p. 273).

V6: **But this *I say*, He that soweth sparingly shall reap also sparingly; and he that soweth bountifully shall reap also bountifully.**

As an incentive to liberality Paul reminds the Corinthians of an unvarying principle, the complete equity of which is immediately apparent; it is that the harvest reaped will be proportionate to the seed sown [cf *Prov* 11.24, 25; *Gal* 6.7–10]. 'They who in giving think, not how little they can give, as they would if self-enrichment were their aim, but of benefits to be conferred, will receive back on the same principle. As they to others, so God will act to them' (Beet).

V7: *Let* **each man** *do* **according as he hath purposed in his heart; not grudgingly, or of necessity: for God loveth a cheerful giver.**

The omission of the verb in the original adds force to the sentence. Each man must be entirely free to decide what he will give, for Paul has every confidence that those who have freely received, will freely give [*Matt* 10.8]. 'There must be real freedom in Christian giving, each individual making the decision in his own heart how much he ought to give. It is far from Paul's intention that a "quota scheme" or a "means test" should be imposed upon the Corinthians' (P. E. Hughes).

not of grief or of necessity: 'Each is to give what he has purposed in his heart, where he is free and true: he is not to give out of grief, mourning over what he gives and regretting he could not keep it; neither is he to give out of necessity, because his position, or the usages of his society, or the comments of his neighbours, put a practical compulsion upon him' (Denney).

for God loveth a cheerful giver. This is taken from the LXX of *Proverbs* 22.8 and gives the general sense of the Hebrew: 'He that hath a bountiful (i.e. a good) eye shall be blessed'. It is the man with a generous eye who delights to devise acts of kindness who is blessed of God. For as Trapp well says, 'One may give with his hand, and pull it back with his looks'. God therefore loves the man who gives joyfully, or with hilarity (*hilaron*)! Then let not 'those who give reluctantly, or from stress of circumstances, or to secure merit, imagine that mere giving is acceptable to God. Unless we feel it is an honour and a joy to give, God does not accept the offering' (Hodge).

*V*8: **And God is able to make all grace abound unto you; that ye, having always all sufficiency in everything, may abound unto every good work:**

The doctrine taught is that abounding grace brings forth abounding good works. The desire to be generous and the means of being generous come from God. So Paul reminds the Corinthians that God is able to make *all* grace abound to them in order that they 'in *all* things at *all* times having *all* sufficiency, may abound to *all* good work' (P. E. Hughes). Paul here gives a Christian meaning to a favourite Stoic word. The inner 'self-sufficiency' of the Stoic made him independent of everything external to himself, but the believer finds his 'self-sufficiency' in the God whose bounty enables him to bestow blessings upon others. 'Enough means not only a sufficiency for oneself but what can also be given to one's brothers. The Christian *self* cannot be considered in isolation. His *self-sufficiency* arises only when the *other* has a share in it' (G. Kittel, *TDNT*, Vol. 1, p. 467).

*V*9: **as it is written,**
  He hath scattered abroad, he hath given to the poor;
  His righteousness abideth for ever.

'Righteousness' here means 'benevolence' (RSV margin). Paul cites *Psalm* 112.9 to prove that a generous-hearted man will never lack the means to express his generosity. 'The man who fears the Lord' and gives to the needy with open-handed beneficence will not be impoverished by his benefactions. His benevolence endures for ever, because God always supplies him with the resources to continue it. Such benevolence is an evidence of righteousness and not a method of attaining it.

*V*10: **And he that supplieth seed to the sower and bread for food, shall supply and multiply your seed for sowing, and increase the fruits of your righteousness:**

and increase the harvest of your benevolence. (RSV margin) The bountiful God who gives 'seed to the sower and bread for food' [*Is* 55.10] will abundantly increase your resources that you may scatter abroad acts of beneficence, as a sower scatters seed. The final clause, which is taken from *Hosea* 10.12 LXX, probably refers 'to the blessings which righteous generosity brings to the giver as well as to the receiver' (Massie).

*V*11: **ye being enriched in everything unto all liberality, which worketh through us thanksgiving to God.**

The proximate purpose for which they are enriched with this wealth is that 'they may exercise a single-mindedness (see on 8.2), which keeps its gaze undistracted by selfish considerations and fixed solely on doing good to the poorer brethren' (Waite). The ultimate purpose is that those benefited will be led to glorify God by their thanksgiving for this liberality which Paul has encouraged ('through us').

*V*12: **For the ministration of this service not only filleth up the measure of the wants of the saints, but aboundeth also through many thanksgivings unto God;**

This expands the thought of the previous verse: for this great public service of ministering to the saints will lead to an overflowing of many thanksgivings to God. 'Paul brings out the distinctive feature of Christian charity. Worldly charity is at best happy only in relieving human distress. Pharisaic and work-righteousness charity thinks it is acquiring merit with God. By relieving distress Christian charity delights in the multiplied thanksgivings that will rise to God from the hearts and the lips of those whose distress is thus relieved' (Lenski).

*V*13: **seeing that through the proving** *of you* **by this ministration they glorify God for the obedience of your confession unto the gospel of Christ, and for the liberality of** *your* **contribution unto them and unto all;**

The saints at Jerusalem would also see in this ministry a proof of the Corinthians' faith and they would glorify God because their confession of the gospel 'finds expression in obedient subjection to its requirements' (Arndt-Gingrich).

and for the single-mindedness of your fellowship with them and with all – (Lenski) Moreover, this tangible proof of the reality of their confession gives evidence of their fellowship not only with the believers in Jerusalem but with all true Christians everywhere. 'Submissive confession of the gospel means single-minded fellowship with all the saints, all of whom so confess and all of whom are in fellowship. The one is never separated from the other. The one is the basis, the other the result. Confession means fellowship, fellowship means confession' (Lenski).

*V*14: **while they themselves also, with supplication on your behalf, long after you by reason of the exceeding grace of God in you.**

Another blessed result of this ministry will be found in the prayers it will lead their Jewish brethren to offer on their behalf, not only on account of the gift itself, but also because of the exceeding grace of God which it shows is resting upon them. For it was 'a moral miracle that Macedonians and Corinthians should be exhibiting such self-sacrifice for Jews' (Goudge). [Rom 15.25, 26]

V15: **Thanks be to God for his unspeakable gift.**

Thanks be to God for his indescribable gift! (NIV) Words fail the apostle as he contemplates the magnitude of that Gift which is beyond all human computation. There is no doubt that the indescribable gift 'for which the apostle bursts out here into a characteristic doxology is the gift of Christ himself [*John* 3.16] and of salvation in him, thankful appreciation of which had borne such fruit in Christian lives' (Bernard).

CHAPTER TEN

Paul, knowing that some Corinthians still disputed his authority, entreats the church not to persist in that disobedience which would force him to take strong measures against them when he came to Corinth [vv 1–6]. His critics should neither judge him by his humble appearance, nor by their own pretensions, since those who scorned his powerful letters would find that his deeds when present were equally powerful [vv 7–11]. Paul refuses to measure himself by the standards of men, for in preaching the gospel to them he has kept within the measure of his divine commission. And though his missionary mandate extends far beyond Corinth, he commends not himself, but glories only in the Lord whose approval he seeks [vv 12–18].

The marked change of tone which is so evident in ch 10–13 has led some scholars to conclude that these chapters are part of the 'severe' letter, but the Epistle is manifestly an intelligible unity as it stands. It is all about Paul's promised visit to Corinth. So if the last four chapters were not written at the same time as the first nine, 'we should not expect to find them take up the matter of the proposed visit just where it is left in ch 9. But this is just what we do find' (Menzies).

In this final part of the Epistle, Paul turns his attention to those who have sown the seeds of dissension in the church at Corinth. False apostles have sought to undermine his authority, and at the same time discredit his gospel, by speaking disparagingly of his 'weakness'. It is therefore entirely natural and eminently sensible that he should answer these attacks and vindicate his apostolic authority before he visits them again. 'The Corinthians must make up their minds, *all* of them, whether Paul is really their apostle or not. There must be no longer any kind of hesitation about this. It is as their apostle by divine commission that he is going to visit them once again, claiming the allegiance that is his due' (Tasker).

*V*1: **Now I Paul myself entreat you by the meekness and gentleness of Christ, I who in your presence am lowly among you, but being absent am of good courage toward you:**

Now I Paul myself This 'is not only the grammatical subject of the sentence, but if one may say so, the subject under consideration; it is the very person whose authority is in dispute who puts himself forward deliberately in this authoritative way' (Denney).

entreat you by the meekness and gentleness of Christ, The apostle cannot have been as ignorant of the Lord's earthly life as some modern scholars imagine, for this appeal assumes a knowledge of the character of Christ which the Corinthians must have owed to his instruction. Paul knows that he is despised for following the example of him whose 'meekness' of heart [*Matt* 11.29] was shown by his 'gentleness' in dealing with poor sinners (e.g. *John* 8.1–11), but he hopes that they will not put his courage to the test! [*v* 2]

I who am humble when face to face with you, but bold to you when I am away! (RSV) This is the only place in the New Testament where 'humble' (*tapeinos*) is used in a bad sense. Paul is echoing the contemptuous accusation of his proud critics who had not learned the Christian meaning of the word. 'They had said that, when he was there, he was a Uriah Heep, very humble and cringing and artful; when he was away from them, he could pluck up his courage and be very resolute – on paper' (Plummer).

V2: **yea, I beseech you, that I may not when present show courage with the confidence wherewith I count to be bold against some, who count of us as if we walked according to the flesh.**

Paul even begs the Corinthians not to force him to display when present that courage which is only attributed to him when absent [13.10]. Indeed he is resolved to act with the greatest boldness against certain persons who wrongly reckon that his conduct is dictated by purely worldly motives. 'His Corinthian detractors judged him by themselves, as if he were influenced by fleshly motives, desire of favour, or fear of offending, so as not to exercise his authority' (Fausset).

V3: **For though we walk in the flesh, we do not war according to the flesh**

Since Paul is a man he is obliged to walk *in* the flesh, but his opponents have greatly misjudged him in thinking that he walks *according to* the flesh. They thought it would be an easy matter to destroy Paul with the carnal weapons in their armoury, but they will shortly discover to their dismay that he neither *walks* nor *wars according to* the flesh. Certainly he will fight these enemies of the gospel to the finish, but not on their terms nor with their weapons [cf *Eph* 6.11–18].

V4: **(for the weapons of our warfare are not of the flesh, but mighty before God to the casting down of strongholds);**

In the spiritual conflict in which Paul was engaged, he placed no reliance in merely human abilities. He had no confidence in fleshly reasonings, arguments, or stratagems, but trusted solely in the supernatural power of God [*Zech* 4.6]. The difficult phrase 'before God' (literally, 'to God') either means that the weapons Paul uses are employed in God's service, or more probably that they are 'divinely potent to demolish strongholds' (NEB). The church must learn that the cause of Christ is never advanced by carnal methods, because the strongholds in which sinners entrench themselves will never yield to the bravest display of worldly weapons. It is only before the resistless power of God that the walls of these fortresses fall flat [*Josh* 6.20].

V5: **casting down imaginations, and every high thing that is exalted against the knowledge of God, and bringing every thought into captivity to the obedience of Christ;**

casting down reasonings, (ASV margin) This warfare is not carnal, for the strongholds that Paul is engaged in demolishing are not the *persons* of the unbelieving, but the sinful *reasonings* – 'the refuge of lies' – by which they seek to fortify themselves against the knowledge of God [cf *Rom* 1.18ff]. The military metaphor 'emphasizes the defiant and mutinous nature of sin: sinful man does not wish to know God; he wishes himself to be the self-sufficient centre of his universe' (P. E. Hughes).

and every high thing that is exalted against the knowledge of God, 'Such were the *high towers* of Judaic self-righteousness, philosophic speculations, and rhetorical sophistries, the "knowledge" so much prized by many, which opposed the "knowledge of God" at Corinth. True knowledge makes men humble. Where self is exalted God is not known' (Fausset).

and bringing every thought into captivity to the obedience of Christ; Such a deliverance from the proud ramparts of 'autonomous' reason has the supremely positive purpose of bringing 'every intention of the mind' (Alford) into subjection to the *obedience of Christ* without which there can be no true *knowledge of God*. But though this is always true of the regenerate in principle, unhappily it is not always so in practice. And Paul intends the Corinthians to see that it was because they had failed fully to submit themselves to the mind of Christ that they 'were being deceived by the specious logic of the false apostles' (P. E. Hughes). [cf 11.2ff]

V6: **and being in readiness to avenge all disobedience, when your obedience shall be made full.**

When Paul at last returns to Corinth those who have charged him with uttering empty threats will find to their dismay that he is more than ready to punish the disobedient. Meanwhile he charitably assumes that the church will act obediently, and so he speaks of '*your* obedience'. But as some will act otherwise, he waits in order to give *all* an opportunity of joining the obedient majority. He will not prematurely exact punishment, but delays his coming 'until the full number of those who obey Christ has been "completed", and the remainder have proved incorrigible' (Fausset).

V7: **Ye look at the things that are before your face. If any man trusteth in himself that he is Christ's, let him consider this again with himself, that, even as he is Christ's, so also are we.**

Look at what is before your eyes. (RSV) It is preferable to take the verb as an imperative. It recalls the Corinthians to reality. If they will but face the facts, they will see that Paul has given them far more convincing evidence of his apostleship than those who have tried so hard to supplant him [cf 1 Cor 9.1, 2].

If any one is confident that he is Christ's, let him remind himself that as he is Christ's, so are we. (RSV) This is an ironical reference to the arrogant claims advanced by his opponents. Should any one regard himself as an apostle of Christ to whom the church at Corinth must defer, let him also consider that Paul's claim to exercise the same authority is no less emphatic than his own. Moreover, in his case this personal conviction can be substantiated with objective credentials which cannot be matched or gainsaid by these wordy claimants to a superior apostleship. [cf 3.2; 11.23–28; 12.12–15]

*V*8: **For though I should glory somewhat abundantly concerning our authority (which the Lord gave for building you up, and not for casting you down), I shall not be put to shame: 9 that I may not seem as if I would terrify you by my letters.**

Paul knows that his critics have accused him of boasting, but even if he were to make higher claims for his ministry he is confident that he would have no cause to be ashamed of his words. He is not like those who must try to bolster up their position with empty boasting, for the reality of his claims is amply borne out by the facts. Because the Lord himself not only appointed him to this office, but his authority as an apostle is always exercised in accordance with the terms of that divine mandate. All his efforts are directed towards the building up of the church, whereas the false apostles used their assumed authority to destroy it. What he says here is no contradiction of verse 5. For though 'we "cast down reasonings", this is not in order to destroy, but to *build up*, by removing hindrances to edification, testing what is unsound, and putting together all that is true in the building'

(Chrysostom cited by Fausset). But Paul refrains from saying anything more about his authority lest he should seem to justify the jibe of his opponents by scaring the Corinthians out of their wits with his letters! A sarcasm which effectively reveals the absurdity of the accusation.

*V*10: **For, His letters, they say, are weighty and strong; but his bodily presence is weak, and his speech of no account.**

It is worth noting that even Paul's detractors were forced to admit that there was nothing weak about his letters. 'The saying is a valuable testimony to the impression the Epistles of Paul at once produced when they were written; they were felt to be grave and important utterances, and they acted effectively, as they were intended to do' (Menzies). It has not since proved necessary to revise this contemporary estimate of the power of Paul's pen.

but his bodily presence is weak, and his speech of no account. They said in effect, 'Paul may write, bold, bluffing letters, but when he appears in person he cannot disguise his weakness and then his speech amounts to nothing!' Thus misjudging Paul's motives, his enemies mistook meekness for weakness [11.21], and branded his artless preaching as being unworthy of the attention of educated Greeks! [11.6; 1 *Cor* 1.17; 2.1–5]

*V*11: **Let such a one reckon this, that, what we are in word by letters when we are absent, such *are we* also in deed when we are present.**

Anyone who is tempted to believe that slander should think again. Let him rather count on the fact that Paul's forthcoming visit will prove that he lacks neither the determination nor the courage to discipline the disobedient. Then it would be evident to all that there was no discrepancy whatever between his words and his deeds [13.2, 10].

*V*12: **For we are not bold to number or compare ourselves with certain of them that commend themselves: but they themselves, measuring themselves by themselves, and comparing themselves with themselves, are without understanding.**

Paul now asks the Corinthians to consider the *character* of the men who have brought such charges against him [*vv* 12–18]. He ironically confesses that he does not have the courage to class or compare himself with certain of those 'who make self-commendation, unsupported by any corroborating evidence, their title to fame' (Tasker). But the self-satisfied are always the self-deluded, for in adopting their own conduct as the standard of excellence, they prove themselves to be devoid of spiritual understanding. Hence their fancied wisdom was in fact arrant folly! 'Instead of the public standard, they measure themselves by one made by themselves: they do not compare themselves with others who excel them, but with those like themselves; hence their high self-esteem. The one-eyed is easily king among the blind' (Fausset). [*Matt* 5.20]

*V*13: **But we will not glory beyond *our* measure, but according to the measure of the province which God apportioned to us as a measure, to reach even unto you.**

It is not for Paul to compete with those who glory only in themselves, though it is not surprising that those who know nothing of God's standard of measurement are well satisfied to measure themselves by themselves. These false apostles would be trespassing wherever they went, for the very 'gospel' [11.4] they preached was an indisputable proof that no sphere of labour had been marked out for them by God. But Paul's glorying is legitimate for he glories in the Lord who called him and who appointed the bounds of his service.

but according to the measure of the province which God apportioned to us as a measure, to reach even unto you. The Judaizers boasted of gifts they did not possess and battened like parasites on churches which they had not founded. Paul did not indulge in such inordinate boasting and it was his settled practice not to build on another man's foundation [*Rom* 15.20]. It was he, and not they, who had brought the gospel as far as Corinth; and since his labours there were the instrumental means of bringing the Corinthians to a living faith in Christ, they of all people ought to be the last to doubt the authority of his apostleship over them [1 *Cor* 9.1, 2].

*V*14: **For we stretch not ourselves overmuch, as though we reached not unto you: for we came even as far as unto you in the gospel of Christ:**

We are not overstretching our commission, as we should be if it did not extend to you, (NEB) The apostle is not the intruder at Corinth; this description applied to the self-appointed interlopers who certainly overstretched themselves by thus encroaching upon a sphere which God had clearly assigned to Paul.

for we were the first to reach Corinth in preaching the gospel of Christ. (NEB) Paul's point is not merely that he was the first to reach Corinth, but that he was the first to reach it with *the gospel of Christ*. For these emissaries of Jewish legalism who had followed him there brought with them 'another gospel which is not another' [*Gal* 1.6, 7]. 'They made it their business to follow in Paul's tracks, to steal into his congregations, and then to undermine his gospel work. They had not even a commission from God, to say nothing of a mark of measurement that had been set by God, which they were to reach. Theirs was the devil's work [11.3, 4]' (Lenski).

*V*15: **not glorying beyond *our* measure, *that is*, in other men's labours; but having hope that, as your faith groweth, we shall be magnified in you according to our province unto *further* abundance, 16. so as to preach the gospel even unto the parts beyond you, *and* not to glory in another's province in regard of things ready to our hand.**

I do not boast beyond due measure by intruding upon a sphere in which others have been commissioned to labour; (Bruce) Paul's 'enemies spoke and acted as if the fruits of his missionary toil had been produced by them. Against this lawless and vaulting ambition he sets his own aspirations' (Waite).

I have good hope that, as your faith increases, my own sphere of labour will be increased the more by your aid, according to the commission which I have been given. That is, I hope to preach the good news in lands farther west than Corinth. (Bruce) He hopes that the Corinthians will help him to fulfil his calling, for it is only when increased faith restores them to full obedience that he will feel free to undertake further responsibilities in claiming new territory for Christ [cf *Rom* 15.18–24]. This shows that the apostle's missionary strategy was based on the sound principle that the consolidation of existing work must precede further advance (Murray Harris).

[131]

But I will not boast beyond due measure by trespassing to someone else's field of labour because it lies ready on my hand. (Bruce) The repetition [cf *v* 15a] 'reveals Paul's deep sense of how unjust is his opponents' boasting. While his thoughts about the Corinthians, whom he had led to Christ, were that their increasing faith would enable him to break up new ground still further off, his opponents were exulting about things in a field allotted by God to Paul, and in reference to work which they found *already done*. With such men Paul dares not compare himself' (Beet).

*V*17: **But he that glorieth, let him glory in the Lord.**

With this quotation of a favourite text Paul puts his own glorying in the right light, and at the same time passes censure upon his opponents [*Jer* 9.23, 24; 1 *Cor* 1.31]. The way in which the New Testament writers freely apply or transfer to Christ references in the Old Testament to Jehovah 'is a significant pointer to the fundamental apostolic belief in the pre-existence of Christ in the unity of the eternal Godhead' (P. E. Hughes).

*V*18: **For not he that commendeth himself is approved, but whom the Lord commendeth.**

Paul has been forced by the attacks made on him to boast about himself, but it was not on this self-praise that he relied. It was ever and only the Lord's approval that he sought, and the manifest blessing which rested upon his work at Corinth and elsewhere proved that he did not lack the tangible tokens of it. The very existence of the Corinthian church was *his* letter of commendation [3.2]. But his 'assailants had no such confirmation of the praise which they bestowed on themselves' (Plummer). In the final analysis all will be constrained to admit that the Lord's commendation is the only one that matters [1 *Cor* 4.3, 4], but those who do not seek to please him *now* will find to their everlasting sorrow and shame that it is too late to do so *then.*

CHAPTER ELEVEN

Although Paul deprecated self-praise, the attacks of the Judaizers forced him to indulge in this folly, lest they should succeed in seducing the Corinthians from their allegiance to Christ by the false gospel they preached [vv 1–4]. That he was not inferior to these superlative apostles was shown not least by his refusal to accept maintenance from the church. This not only proved his love, but also demonstrated how he differed from the false apostles who gloried only in the guise they assumed [vv 5–15]. Since Paul must boast, he will not exalt himself after the manner of those who would bring them into bondage, but will glory only in his sufferings. He is also a Jew, but the badges of his office consist in his labours, hardships, and the daily burden of his care for the churches. Hence Paul glories in that weakness which began at Damascus when the converted persecutor became the persecuted apostle [vv 16–33].

VI: **Would that ye could bear with me in a little foolishness: but indeed ye do bear with me.**

Paul finds it distasteful to boast about himself, but the tactics of his rivals are forcing him to descend to their level. If he now assumes the fool's mask for a little while, it is because his concern for the Corinthians leads him to expose the folly that is so entirely natural to the men who had deceived them with their great swelling words. In this chapter he sweeps aside the empty boasting of these vocal pretenders to the apostolate with a devastating revelation of what it cost him to be faithful to his commission. With magnificent irony Paul begins by wishing that the Corinthians would bear with him in a little of the folly of self-boasting! But he immediately corrects himself, for after all, such an appeal is quite super-fluous when they are so practised 'in enduring the overbearing demeanour of his opponents! [*v* 20]. (Massie).

*V*2: **For I am jealous over you with a godly jealousy: for I espoused you to one husband, that I might present you *as* a pure virgin to Christ.**

'This is why he plays the fool', says Calvin, 'for jealousy sweeps a man off his feet'. But the jealousy Paul feels is not for himself or his own reputation, it is a jealousy he endures on God's behalf. His feelings towards the Corinthians are in certain respects analogous to those of Jehovah over faithless Israel [*Hos* 2.19, 20; 4.12]. For as their spiritual father [1 *Cor* 4.15], he has betrothed them to one husband, but he is begin-ning to be fearful for the purity of the prospective bride. 'It is necessary that the bride should concentrate her attention on the "one man" to whom she is engaged, and not open her heart to any other; but there is reason to fear that the Corin-thian church is having its attention distracted from the true object, namely, from Christ as he was preached by Paul. He is afraid that this bride is allowing other views to be introduced into her mind, views inconsistent with her first loyalty' (Menzies).

that I might present you *as* a pure virgin to Christ. 'As, in *Eph* 5. 27, this presentation of the church to Christ as his bride, is said to take place at his second coming, this passage is commonly understood to refer to that event. Paul's desire was that the Corinthians should remain faithful to their vows, so as to be presented to Christ a glorious church, without spot or wrinkle, on that great day. He dreaded lest they should, in that day, be rejected and contemned as a woman unfaithful to her vows' (Hodge).

*V*3: **But I fear, lest by any means, as the serpent beguiled Eve in his craftiness, your minds should be corrupted from the simplicity and the purity that is toward Christ.**

Although many of the best manuscripts add 'and purity', this was probably suggested by 'pure' in verse 2 (Barrett). 'Simplicity' [cf 8.2] refers to the single-minded devotion that the church should have towards Christ. 'What Paul dreads is the spiritual seduction of the church, the winning away of her heart from absolute loyalty to Christ. The serpent beguiled Eve by his craftiness; he took advantage of her unsuspecting innocence to wile her away from her simple belief in God and obedience to him . . . The serpent's agents – the servants of Satan, as Paul calls them in verse 15 – are at work in Corinth; and he fears that their craftiness may seduce the church from its first simple loyalty to Christ' (Denney). [*Gen* 3.13]

*V*4: **For if he that cometh preacheth another Jesus, whom we did not preach, or *if* ye receive a different spirit, which ye did not receive, or a different gospel, which ye did not accept, ye do well to bear with *him*.**

When the Corinthians bear with the false apostles so well, they should not find it too difficult to put up with their genuine apostle for a little while! 'If' denotes a condition of reality. Paul does not point to any imaginary danger but describes the actual situation in Corinth. Here the actions of one false teacher are representative of all who are like him. He comes of his own volition, as opposed to being commissioned and sent by God [*vv* 13–15]. These men 'had simply *come*, unsent and without divine authorization; and therefore they were no apostles' (P. E. Hughes).

preacheth another Jesus, whom we did not preach, Paul consigns to a decent oblivion the precise nature of his opponents' teaching, but it is hardly likely that he would have overlooked a defective Christology without comment. On this assumption the contrast would not be between their human Jesus and his heavenly Christ. It would seem a far more reasonable surmise to suggest that in transforming the gospel into a scheme of salvation by works, these Jewish legalists in effect preached 'another Jesus' even though they held to an orthodox view of his Person, including the confession of his Deity.

or *if* ye receive a different spirit, which ye did not receive. An ironical allusion to the powerlessness of the Judaizers to impart the Holy Spirit. They are dispensers of a different spirit, a spirit which is consonant with the doctrine taught. It is the spirit 'which gendereth to bondage' [*Gal* 4.24, 25; 5.1, 4].

or a different gospel, which ye did not accept, It was in connection with Paul's preaching of Jesus as the *Saviour* of sinners that the Corinthians received the Spirit through whom they were able to accept the *one* authentic gospel. 'The will of man is passive in RECEIVING the "Spirit"; but it is actively concurrent with the will of God (which goes before to give the good will) in ACCEPTING the "Gospel"' (Fausset). But to give heed to a man who preaches *another* Jesus is to receive a *different* spirit and to accept a *different* gospel!

you put up with it well enough! (Arndt-Gingrich) A cutting reflection on their disloyalty to him. '*He* had to plead for their toleration, but they had no difficulty in tolerating men who by a spurious gospel, an unspiritual conception of Christ, and an unworthy incapacity for understanding freedom, were undermining his work, and seducing their souls' (Denney).

*V*5: **For I reckon that I am not a whit behind the very chiefest apostles.**

for I reckon that I am in nothing behind the superlative apostles! (Waite) It is difficult to believe that Paul would speak so scathingly of the Jerusalem apostles; his scorn is directed at the Judaizers who presumably claimed *their* authority to propagate a *different* gospel [*v* 4]. 'What a pity you find it so easy to tolerate these superfine apostles when my credentials are in no way inferior to theirs!' Paul is not seriously comparing himself with the *false* apostles [*v* 13], 'but speaking with incisive bitterness of the supposed position of inferiority which they had tried to assign to him' (Waite).

*V*6: **But though *I be* rude in speech, yet *am I* not in knowledge; nay, in every way have we made *this* manifest unto you in all things.**

This concession to the criticism of his enemies is also tinged with irony. If Paul's speech was devoid of the ornamental flourishes of a man trained in the art of rhetoric, its content was certainly not deficient in knowledge as the Corinthians had good cause to know [cf 1 *Cor* 2]. But it is the mark of an infantile mind to be more concerned with the wrappings than the contents of the parcel! Unlike the pretenders to apostolic status, Paul possesses a divine commission to manifest the truth to every man's conscience [4.2]. He has made known this knowledge without the slightest reserve, freely declaring the whole counsel of God to all who would listen to him.

*V*7: **Or did I commit a sin in abasing myself that ye might be exalted, because I preached to you the gospel of God for nought?**

Or perhaps the Corinthians prefer these false gospellers because they have had to pay for the privilege of being deceived by them? Evidently Paul's opponents had said that his refusal to accept maintenance from the Corinthians was a tacit admission of his amateur status, for a proper apostle would have received it as a right! [*v* 12; cf 1 *Cor* 9.4–19]. 'Christ's pure Gospel without price and the corrupted doctrine of the Judaizers at a cost [11.20]; his self-abasement and their self-glorification; his emancipation and their enslaving of the community, are pointed contrasts' (Waite).

*V*8: **I robbed other churches, taking wages *of them* that I might minister unto you;**

Paul even 'robbed' other churches, i.e. 'accepting support so that I might serve you' (Arndt-Gingrich). He accepted a subsistence from the poorer Macedonian churches, which were not receiving the benefits of his ministry, in order that he might minister the gospel without charge to the Corinthians. Paul rubs in this truth and makes it smart 'to drive out their mean ingratitude. For what is meaner than to slander a benefactor for bestowing his benefaction *gratis*?' (Lenski).

*V*9: **and when I was present with you and was in want, I was not a burden on any man; for the brethren, when they came from Macedonia, supplied the measure of my want; and in everything I kept myself from being burdensome unto you, and *so* will I keep *myself*.**

While ministering to the Corinthians Paul ran short of funds, probably because the demands they made on him meant that he could not work long enough at his trade to support himself [*Acts* 18.3]. Yet even then no one found him a 'burden' – a word derived from *narkē*, the torpedo fish which benumbs anyone who touches it; 'hence to be idle to the detriment of another person (like a useless limb)' (Vine) – for his needs were met by the unstinted generosity of the brethren from Macedonia. Thus during the whole of his mission to Corinth Paul studiously avoided taking any financial assistance from the Corinthians, and whatever the mercenary-minded Judaizers might say about it, he would maintain this independence on his forthcoming visit.

*V*10: **As the truth of Christ is in me, no man shall stop me of this glorying in the regions of Achaia.**

Paul, conscious of the fact that he speaks in conformity with the truthfulness of Christ, here avers that 'this boasting will not (let itself) be stopped' (Arndt-Gingrich). Despite the desperate attempts of his enemies to stop (i.e. to block by barricade or damming up) the flow of his boasting about preaching without payment, they will not succeed either in Corinth or indeed throughout all Achaia.

*V*11: **Wherefore? because I love you not? God knoweth.**
It would seem that the false apostles had insinuated it was because Paul cared so little for the Corinthians that he refused to take their money, whereas *they* had enough affection for them to receive it! Can they really find it in their hearts to believe that he is too proud to be indebted to those to whom he is indifferent? If they did not know him better than that, there is One who does. God, before whom no secrets are hid, takes full cognizance of the strength of his feeling for them, and knows the real reason for his refusal to accept their support.

[140]

*V*12: **But what I do, that I will do, that I may cut off occasion from them that desire an occasion; that wherein they glory, they may be found even as we.**

And I will keep on doing what I am doing in order to cut the ground from under those who want an opportunity to be considered equal with us in the things they boast about. (NIV) Paul's rivals will be disappointed if they hope that their criticism of his disinterestedness will induce him to follow their lead in accepting money from the Corinthians. For he is determined not to afford them any pretext for claiming that their nefarious work of deception has even a semblance of equality with the authentic ministry which he exercises. 'Paul was too capable a strategist to surrender such a position to the enemy. It would never be by any action of his that he and they found themselves on the same ground' (Denney).

*V*13: **For such men are false apostles, deceitful workers, fashioning themselves into apostles of Christ.**

Not a few have questioned the apostle's wisdom in using such 'intemperate' language, but as Bengel finely observes, 'the Indifferentism, which is so pleasant to many in the present day, was not cultivated by Paul. He was no pleasant preacher of toleration'. But the truth is always intolerable to those who are distinguished by their easy toleration of every conceivable deviation from the faith 'once for all delivered unto the saints' [*Jude* 3]. Today when every babbler of error is almost certain to be hailed as an apostle of Christ by a degenerate Christianity, it is high time for those who remain faithful to the testimony of Jesus to sound no uncertain note of warning. The moment is long overdue for professed Evangelicals to stop fêting the traducers of their Lord and to recognize these men for the deceitful workers they are.

fashioning themselves into apostles of Christ. They changed their outward appearance by assuming the guise of Christ's servants, but their essential character as the slaves of Satan remained unchanged. 'They pose as something which they are not, and in doing so they deceive those who through gullibility or inexperience are more ready to give credence to plausible imposters than to remember the sound teaching and warnings of him who is their true apostle' (P. E. Hughes).

*V*14: **And no marvel; for even Satan fashioneth himself into an angel of light.**

It is no wonder that those who are in reality opposed to Christ should wish to be taken for his apostles, for in this they are merely following the practice of their true master! Satan's masquerading by deceit as a messenger of light, i.e. as the herald of true knowledge, is but the pattern of his conduct as the deceiver, from his first dealings with mankind in the Garden of Eden [*v* 3]. Because it is only by posing as the champion of truth that the prince of darkness is able to persuade men to swallow his lies.

'Satan is most hurtful to the church, when he opposes it by subtlety and creeping; when he comes not as an open enemy, but an appearing friend. He is never so much a devil, as when he appears in white, and transforms himself into an angel of light. He does more hurt by creeping into, than breaking into, the church. False apostles and seducers in the church have been more hurtful to it by fraud, than bloody and paganish persecutors by force. Satan has gained more victories by using the one as sunshine to dazzle the eyes, than by raising the other as wind to blow in the faces of the faithful' (William Jenkyn, *The Epistle of Jude,* p. 78).

*V*15: **It is no great thing therefore if his ministers also fashion themselves as ministers of righteousness; whose end shall be according to their works.**

It is therefore no great thing, 'if Satan's power to present himself in a guise foreign to his real nature should also be be found in those enlisted in his service. Appearing as *the ministers of righteousness,* i.e. eloquent advocates of the Pharisaic doctrine that men can put themselves right with God by their own unaided efforts, they are in fact deceivers of others because they are themselves deceived' (Tasker). [cf *Acts* 13.39; *Rom* 10.3; *Gal* 2.21; *Phil* 3.6, 9] But their end will be according to their Satanic deeds, and not according to their apostolic pretensions! [5.10]. Then those who thought that they were saved by 'works' will discover to their eternal confusion that these were not sufficient to secure them a place among the redeemed.

*V*16: **I say again, Let no man think me foolish; but if** *ye do*, **yet as foolish receive me, that I also may glory a little.**

In returning to the theme of 'boasting', Paul again makes clear his extreme reluctance to indulge in the same folly as the Judaizers [*v* 1]. He wishes the Corinthians to understand that though such boasting is natural to the false apostles, he is only acting a part which has been forced upon him by their accusations. But if they insist on regarding him as a fool, then let them *also* listen to a little of *his* foolishness. After all, this should be no hardship to those who are so ready to welcome fools with open arms!

*V*17: **That which I speak, I speak not after the Lord, but as in foolishness, in this confidence of glorying.**

I speak not after the Lord To regard this as a disclaimer of either the authority or the inspiration of the Lord is not only to discount the value of Paul's utterance for the church but also to do him a grave injustice. Lenski brings out the true meaning of the verse: 'This foolish boasting will not follow the norm and principle of Jesus, for it will be done, not, indeed, "*in* folly", yet "*as in* folly". It will look like folly. It will thus stoop to a lower norm than Jesus used. If it were done in actual folly it would, of course, be stooping to sin; since it is done only in apparent folly it is not sin but is ethically on a lower plane than the one on which Jesus moved'. This explains why Paul is so reluctant to glory, but he is going to do so in order to bring the Corinthians to their senses.

*V*18: **Seeing that many glory after the flesh, I will glory also.**

After the flesh here means to 'boast of one's outward circumstances, i.e. descent, manner of life, etc. [cf *v* 22]' (Arndt-Gingrich). Since his opponents wax eloquent in extolling their external advantages, Paul will meet them on the same ground to show the Corinthians that even at this low level of boasting he is not a whit behind these superlative apostles! [*v* 5].

*V*19: **For ye bear with the foolish gladly, being wise** *yourselves.*

foolish ... being wise 'The Greek antithesis is "senseless, sensible". The irony cuts at the Corinthian self-sufficiency, which blinds them to what real folly is. "Foolish are these boasters; but you plume yourselves on your shrewdness in accepting them. So you will, I am sure, accept me when I talk like them" ' (Massie).

*V*20: **For ye bear with a man, if he bringeth you into bondage, if he devoureth you, if he taketh you *captive*, if he exalteth himself, if he smiteth you on the face.**

Paul knows that the Corinthians will put up with *him* when they are so patiently enduring the indignities which are being heaped upon them by these tyrannical teachers! Not only have they suffered these things, for all the 'ifs' denote reality, 'but the conditional form also implies that they are ready to have it repeated again and again' (Lenski).

1. They were being enslaved. In forfeiting Christian liberty for the yoke of Jewish legalism, they were exchanging their spiritual freedom for abject bondage [*Gal* 2.4; 5.1].

2. They were being exploited. 'Devours' vividly describes the rapacious exactions of the Judaizers which they justified on the grounds of apostolic rights! [cf *Luke* 20.47].

3. They were being ensnared. This word pictures them as caught by the crafty cunning of these unscrupulous hunters of the souls of men.

4. They were being dominated. The false apostles made free use of their usurped authority to lord it over the Corinthians.

5. They were being humiliated. To crown it all, it would seem that their new masters even resorted to physical violence. This was doubtless done 'under the pretext of divine zeal. The height of insolence on their part, and of servile endurance on yours [1 *Kings* 22.24; *Neh* 13.25; *Luke* 22.64; *Acts* 23.2; 1 *Tim* 3.3)' (Fausset).

*V*21a: **I speak by way of disparagement, as though we had been weak.**

To my shame I admit that we were too weak for that! (NIV) This final shaft brings Paul's biting satire to a shattering climax. He might well have said, 'What a disgrace *for you* to have received such fellows *gladly*!' Instead he says, 'No, the

disgrace is mine, for *we* were too *weak* to treat you like that!'
[cf 10.10]. Yes, these 'false apostles know how real apostles
ought to act so as to impress you with what real apostles are;
we – why, we did not even know how to act as apostles'
(Lenski). This makes the Corinthians realize the full shame of
their disloyalty as nothing else would.

*V*21b: **Yet whereinsoever any is bold (I speak in foolishness), I am bold also.**

Paul's lengthy preamble is over. Although the task is dis-
agreeable, the moment has come when for the sake of the
Corinthians he must cast modesty aside and launch into his
'foolish' boasting. This he does in the full confidence that he
is well able to match any claim put forward by his rivals. For
'the grounds on which they show their audacity are as much
mine as theirs' (Massie).

*V*22: **Are they Hebrews? so am I. Are they Israelites?
so am I. Are they the seed of Abraham? so am I.**

That Paul should place this proud claim in the forefront of
his apology would seem to indicate that his antagonists were
Palestinian Jews who boasted of the purity of their descent in
order to confine the Corinthians within the straitjacket of
their Judaistic 'gospel'. But he insists that his own pedigree is
in no sense inferior to theirs; he has inherited exactly the
same privileges, though of course he attached a very different
value to them [cf *Rom* 4.9–18]. The three questions form a
climax, – ' "Hebrews" referring to the *language* and *nation-
ality*; "Israelites", to the *theocracy* and *descent from Israel*, the
"prince who prevailed with God" [*Rom* 9.4]; "the seed of
Abraham", to the *claim to a share in the Messiah* [*Rom* 9.7;
11.1]. Cf *Phil* 3.5, "an Hebrew of the Hebrews"; not an

Hellenist or Greek-speaking Jew, but a Hebrew in tongue, sprung from Hebrews' (Fausset).

*V*23: **Are they ministers of Christ? (I speak as one beside himself) I more; in labours more abundantly, in prisons more abundantly, in stripes above measure, in deaths oft.**

Are they ministers of Christ? . . . I more; 'i.e. I am more a minister of Christ than they, not I am more than a minister of Christ. "The more a man suffers", says Bengel. "the more he ministers" ' (Goudge). As a minister of Christ Paul is far beyond them, because they are not ministers of Christ *at all* [*vv* 13, 15]; so here he does not say 'So am I'.

(I speak as one beside himself) Paul thus interrupts his boasting, because he knows that 'to glory about so sacred a matter as the service of Christ is downright madness' (Plummer).

through hard toils in abundance, through imprisonments in abundance, through stripes beyond measure, through deadly perils on many occasions (Massie) The reality of Paul's ministry is so completely beyond the empty claims of the false apostles that no comparison between them is possible. They had brought letters of commendation [3.1], but he bears on his body 'the marks of Jesus' [*Gal* 6.17]. Paul finds the badges of his office in what he has suffered for Christ, but the Judaizers are mere verbalizers. They have no such credentials to offer.

*V*24: **Of the Jews five times received I forty *stripes* save one.**

[147]

Paul's revealing account of the terrible sufferings he had endured up to the time of writing this Epistle conveys a vivid impression of his extraordinary labours and forms a valuable supplement to the very selective outline of his life in Acts. On no less than five occasions he was sentenced by the Jews to be beaten within an inch of his life. Forty strokes was the maximum punishment which could be inflicted short of the death penalty [*Deut* 25.3], and this was later reduced to thirty-nine for fear of a miscount. 'Notice that the Jews, even in cruelty and injustice to a servant of God, were scrupulously careful to obey in an insignificant detail the letter of the Law. Cf *Matt* 23.23' (Beet). [*Matt* 10.17]

*V*25: **Thrice was I beaten with rods, once was I stoned, thrice I suffered shipwreck, a night and a day have I been in the deep;**

Of the three occasions when Paul was beaten by the Roman authorities we only have a record of the one at Philippi [*Acts* 16.22, 23, 37]. As Plummer points out, the fact that Paul 'was thrice treated in this way is evidence that being a Roman citizen was an imperfect protection when magistrates were disposed to be brutal'. Although Luke gives an account of the stoning at Lystra [*Acts* 14.19], he does not mention these shipwrecks, which of course took place before that recorded in *Acts* 27, but Paul made many voyages – P. E. Hughes calculates at least eighteen – and sailing was a risky business in those days.

a night and a day I have been adrift at sea; (RSV) This means that Paul was in (not under) the sea, probably clinging to some fragment of the wreck, in imminent peril of his life for twenty-four hours before being rescued. The tense may indicate that a recent experience is here vividly recalled.

*V*26: *in* **journeyings often,** *in* **perils of rivers,** *in* **perils of robbers,** *in* **perils from** *my* **countrymen,** *in* **perils from the Gentiles,** *in* **perils in the city,** *in* **perils in the wilderness,** *in* **perils in the sea,** *in* **perils among false brethren;**

A graphic description of the many hazards Paul continually faced in the prosecution of his apostolic commission, of which the last would be the most distressing [cf *Gal* 2.4 where the same word is used of the Judaizers). The pseudo-apostles also braved the dangers of first-century travel to reach Corinth with their false gospel, but none of *their* perils were like Paul's. 'Paul's were perils that were met with on *apostolic* journeys, theirs were perils such as the Pharisees encountered when they compassed sea and land to make one proselyte; "and when he is made, ye make him two-fold more the child of hell than yourselves", *Matt* 23.15' (Lenski). How like the cultists today!

*V*27: *in* **labour and travail, in watchings often, in hunger and thirst, in fastings often, in cold and nakedness.**

I have laboured and toiled and have often gone without sleep; I have known hunger and thirst and have often gone without food; I have been cold and naked. (NIV) In addition to these perils, the physical privations Paul endured would have served to quench the ardour of a less indomitable spirit than his. The 'fastings' referred to here were not religious, though they were voluntary in the sense that Paul often went without food because his work left him no time to eat. 'When we remember that he who endured all this was a man constantly suffering from infirm health [4.7–12; 12. 7–10; *Gal* 4.13, 14], such heroic self-devotion seems almost superhuman' (Conybeare and Howson).

*V*28: **Besides those things that are without, there is that which presseth upon me daily, anxiety for all the churches.**

It is more likely that the opening phrase means: 'besides the things that I do not mention' (Plummer). Paul could say much more along the same lines, but he wants the troublesome church in Corinth to understand that all these trials are as nothing compared with the daily pressure of his anxiety for all the churches. He regards this as his real burden; his other troubles are only the incidental extras he receives by way of a bonus! His evaluation is intended to startle the Corinthians, especially when it is contrasted with the callous indifference of the selfish hirelings they had been so ready to welcome as their true shepherds.

*V*29: **Who is weak, and I am not weak? who is caused to stumble, and I burn not?**

Paul's deep concern for the churches leads him to sympathize with the weak and to wax indignant against their seducers. He feels their weakness as though it were his own. Christian love is gentle and bears patiently with the weak, but carnal pride ruthlessly takes advantage of their weakness to impose its own will on them. Thus the weak Corinthians had succumbed to the boastful strength of the Judaizers!

If anyone is made to stumble, does my heart not blaze with indignation? (NEB) 'It was not to Paul a matter of indifference when any of the brethren, by the force of evil example, or by the seductions of false teachers, were led to depart from the truth or to act inconsistently with their profession. Such events filled him not only with grief at the fall of the weak, but with indignation at the authors of their fall' (Hodge).

*V*30: **If I must needs glory, I will glory of the things that concern my weakness.**

This verse looks both ways. It sums up what has gone before [*vv* 23–28], and is the preface to what follows [12.5–10]. Paul had promised to join his adversaries in the foolishness of boasting, but his boasting has been of a very different character from theirs. For he does not boast of his achievements, but always of the things that concern his weakness. 'He set out to boast; see how he has done it! he has brought forward the very things a boastful person would have said nothing about. There is a boast for you! The Corinthians, carried away by the boasting of those other people, are now to look at this boast too, and see what they think of it' (Menzies).

*V*31: **The God and Father of the Lord Jesus, he who is blessed for evermore knoweth that I lie not.**

This solemn assurance vouches for the veracity of all that he has said and all that he has yet to say concerning his weakness, and was doubtless intended to counter the calumnies which were circulated about the reliability of his word [1.17]. As befits the servant of the One who cannot lie, Paul speaks only what God *knows* to be the truth [cf *Rom* 9.5 and see comment on 1.3].

*V*32: **In Damascus the governor under Aretas the king guarded the city of the Damascenes in order to take me: 33 and through a window was I let down in a basket by the wall, and escaped his hands.**

Many have wondered why Paul should have decided to mention his escape from Damascus at this particular point. The most reasonable explanation would seem to be that this experience marked the beginning of his 'weakness'. The name of

Damascus was indelibly engraved upon the tablet of his memory because it was 'there that the persecutor became the persecuted' (Waite). What a contrast there was between his arrogant approach to the city, and his humiliating exit from it! [cf *Acts* 9.1, 2, 23–25] Moreover, this account of Paul's inglorious escape is also in pointed contrast to the experience which he is about to describe [12.2ff]. 'The man who experienced the ineffable "ascent" even to the third heaven was the same man who had experienced the undistinguished "descent" from a window in the Damascus wall' (P. E. Hughes).

Damascus was not part of the Nabataean kingdom which bordered it, but the governor (or ethnarch) of King Aretas had jurisdiction over the large Arabian colony in the city. In seeking to silence a notorious troublemaker, the Jews successfully enlisted the help of the governor who made arrangements for his clandestine arrest. 'The ethnarch had no authority to arrest Saul openly, as he would have had if Damascus had at this time been part of Aretas's realm' (F. F. Bruce, *Commentary on the Book of Acts,* p. 204).

CHAPTER TWELVE

Paul here discloses that though he had been favoured with inex-
pressible revelations, yet he chose rather to glory in his weaknesses
in case any man accounted him to be above that which could be seen
and heard [vv 1–6]. To prevent his being filled with pride by these
proofs of God's favour, he was given a painful affliction from which
he thrice prayed to be delivered. But instead of granting his request,
the Lord assured him that the power of his grace is made perfect in
man's weakness. Therefore he gladly glories in his weaknesses that
the power of Christ may rest upon him [vv 7–10]. Paul blames the
Corinthians for forcing him to become a fool by boasting when they
had been given ample proofs of his apostleship. If they were less
privileged than other churches, it was only in his refusal to be a
burden to them [vv 11–13]. Before he comes on his third visit he
assures them of his unchanging affection, and reminds them that
they are well qualified to rebut the attacks which have been made
on his integrity [vv 14–18]. But he fears lest when he comes he
should find many grave disorders still unresolved, to his sorrow
and theirs [vv 19–21].

V1: **I must needs glory, though it is not expedient; but
I will come to visions and revelations of the Lord.**

I am obliged to boast. (NEB) Paul introduces his final boast
with a fresh apology. Such boasting is not delightful, but it
is necessary. It is with the greatest reluctance that he brings

forward an experience about which he has kept silent for fourteen years, and the only reason he does so now is in order to relate its sequel [vv 7–10]. Hence his purpose is again to reduce his boast to a 'boasting in weakness' (Massie).

It does no good; (NEB) i.e. it is not useful or helpful. 'He means that he expects to confer no spiritual profit upon the Corinthians by telling them about this phenomenal experience of his' (Lenski).

but I shall go on to tell of visions and revelations granted by the Lord. (NEB) The construction indicates the Lord as the source of the visions and revelations. The plural indicates that Paul is no stranger to those ecstatic experiences of which the super-apostles had evidently boasted to the Corinthians. Of the many revelations vouchsafed to him, he selects one that marked a turning-point in his life, yet what he heard clearly impressed him more than anything he may have seen [v 4]. The visions Paul received had a revelatory function, but not every revelation that was made to him was visually mediated.[1]

---

1. *It is important for Christians today to grasp the fact that the gospel would be incomplete if extra-Biblical revelations were necessary to supplement its teaching.* Revelation is the interpretation of a redemption which is partly objective and partly subjective. Revelation keeps pace with the *objective acts* of redemption, the incarnation, the atonement, and the resurrection of Christ, but it does not accompany the *subjective application* of that redemption to the individual in regeneration, conversion, justification, and sanctification. This explains why redemption extends further than revelation. To insist upon revelation 'accompanying subjective-individual redemption would imply that it dealt with questions of private personal concern, instead of with the common concerns of the world of redemption collectively' (condensed and quoted from *Biblical Theology* by Geerhardus Vos, p. 14). This means that inspiration, in the full apostolic meaning of the word, ceased when the canon of Scripture was brought to completion. Without such *apostolic*

V2: **I know a man in Christ, fourteen years ago (whether in the body, I know not; or whether out of the body, I know not; God knoweth), such a one caught up even to the third heaven.**

The man Paul knows intimately is of course himself, but he chooses to speak in the third person to avoid the appearance of boasting in what he is now forced to relate [*vv* 5, 6]. 'Another person might shout: '*I, I,* have been in Paradise!' and exalt himself above all his fellow men. Another man might tell about it on every possible occasion. Paul kept it a secret for fourteen years' (Lenski). As this Epistle was written in AD 56, fourteen years before would mean that this took place around AD 43, possibly towards the end of Paul's sojourn at Tarsus [*Acts* 9.30; 11.25]. If so, the experience would have inwardly prepared him to obey the outward call of Barnabas to engage in the momentous work of preaching to the Gentiles at Antioch [*Acts* 11.16; cf *Acts* 10.9–29].

(whether in the body, I know not; or whether out of the body, I know not; God knoweth), 'Ignorance of the mode does not take away the certain knowledge of the thing' (Bengel). Since Paul confessed his ignorance as to whether he was in or out of the body at the time, speculation on the matter is quite pointless, for we can hardly expect to establish what he himself was unable to determine. What satisfied him, should satisfy us too: '*God* knoweth'.

---

inspiration there can be no *infallible* revelation. The only revelation from God which Christians still await is the Revelation of Jesus Christ at his second Coming. And that will be objective enough to satisfy everyone that it has really taken place! See also 'The Finality and Sufficiency of Scripture' in *Collected Writings of John Murray*, Vol. I (Banner of Truth, 1976), and the Chapter 'Is Scripture Complete?' in Walter Chantry's *Signs of the Apostles* (Banner of Truth, 1976).

such an one caught up 'The same word describes how surviving Christians will be "caught up" to meet the descending Lord [1 *Thess* 4.17]' (Massie).

even to the third heaven. As Calvin sensibly remarks, Paul is not here drawing fine philosophical distinctions between the different heavens, but uses three as a perfect number to indicate what is highest and most complete. Thus 'not content with using the simple word heaven, Paul adds that he had reached its utmost height and innermost chambers'.

*V*3: **And I know such a man (whether in the body, or apart from the body, I know not; God knoweth), 4 how that he was caught up into Paradise, and heard unspeakable words, which it is not lawful for a man to utter.**

The solemn repetition in verse 3 prepares the way for some additional information about the same experience. Although Paul offers no description of Paradise, he knows he has been there. The first Paradise in Eden was 'lost' through sin, but through the triumph of grace that lost glory is 'regained' in the Paradise of heaven [cf *Luke* 23.43; *Rev* 2.7]. What Paul heard was incommunicable, but he preached an intelligible message of salvation. 'Paul was not a "gnostic", but a witness; salvation, according to his teaching, came not through a mystic vision, but through the hearing of faith' (J. G. Machen, *The Origin of Paul's Religion*, p. 265).

which it is not lawful for a man to utter. 'If anyone retorts that in that case what Paul heard was superfluous and useless, for what good was there in hearing something that had to be held back in perpetual silence, my answer is that this thing happened for Paul's own sake, for a man who had awaiting him troubles hard enough to break a thousand hearts needed to be strengthened in a special way to keep him from giving way and to help him to persevere undaunted' (Calvin).

*V*5: **On behalf of such a one will I glory: but on mine own behalf I will not glory, save in *my* weaknesses.**

'On behalf of one, who in all this was entirely passive and recipient, without exertion or merit of his own, he will boast, but not on behalf of his personal self, his own will, work and service, except with regard to his infirmities. He has already in mind the infirmity of verse 7; the correlative of his visions and revelations' (Waite).

*V*6: **For if I should desire to glory, I shall not be foolish; for I shall speak the truth: but I forbear, lest any man should account of me above that which he seeth me *to be*, or heareth from me.**

If I should choose to boast, it would not be the boast of a fool, for I should be speaking the truth. (NEB) Paul cuts short his glorying even though he could say a great deal more, all of which would be nothing but the sober truth. 'Even in his great humility Paul takes care to leave no false impressions. He *was* something by the grace of God [1 *Cor* 15.10]. It would be falsehood to deny it even by implication, an implication which one might falsely deduce from the emphasis which Paul puts on his weakness as being his only boast' (Lenski).

But I refrain, because I should not like anyone to form an estimate of me which goes beyond the evidence of his own eyes and ears. (NEB) It is significant that Paul thus refuses to make mystical experience a ground for claiming apostolic authority, when his opponents had clearly made much of their imaginary visions to enhance their standing in Corinth. 'Paul places no such value on ecstasy, nor does he imply that he was nearer to God then – when caught up into Paradise – than at other times under normal conditions. This is an important observation, which should set us on our guard against all forms of "mysticism" and exceptional experiences which are made the basis for some claim in a matter of Christian doctrine or practice' (Ralph P. Martin, *Daily Bible Commentary*, Vol. 4, p. 200).

V7: **And by reason of the exceeding greatness of the revelations, that I should not be exalted overmuch, there was given to me a thorn in the flesh, a messenger of Satan to buffet me, that I should not be exalted overmuch.**

It should not be forgotten that self-deification is the great goal of fallen man [*Gen* 3.5], and even believers need to be protected against assuming that their spiritual privileges are their own prerogatives. 'How dangerous must self-exaltation be, when the apostle required so much restraint!' (Bengel).

there was given to me a thorn in the flesh, The gift was entirely unsolicited by Paul, but with the gift he was also given the grace to receive it as a favour! Of this 'thorn' we know no more than Paul tells us here. That it was a recurring painful physical affliction is certain, but an exact diagnosis of the condition is impossible. Our ignorance remains even if *Gal* 4.13, 14 may be legitimately linked with this verse. The most plausible guesses all fall short of final certainty. If it had been spiritually profitable for us to know the nature of this malady God would have told us. As it is, Paul's thorn in the flesh becomes 'by its very lack of definition, a type of every Christian's "thorn in the flesh", not with regard to externals, but by its spiritual significance' (P. E. Hughes).

a messenger of Satan to buffet me, The case of Job furnishes a helpful parallel [*Job* 2.7], for it shows that it was within God's wise and holy purpose to prove the fidelity of his servant by sending Satan to do the evil work in which he takes a fiendish delight [cf *Luke* 13.16]. Satan could not touch a hair of Job's head without leave, for absolutely nothing lies outside the scope of God's sovereignty. All God's creatures are subject to his ruling and over-ruling; and even the work of Satan is overruled so that it assists in bringing to pass the divine purpose, though Satan on his part uses his utmost powers to thwart that purpose.

that I should not be exalted overmuch. The divine purpose in this affliction is repeated for emphasis. Satan's malice is always frustrated by God and made to minister a blessing *to his people*. The 'all things' of *Rom* 8.28 admits of no exceptions.

*V*8: **Concerning this thing I besought the Lord thrice, that it might depart from me.**

On three occasions Paul made it a matter of earnest entreaty that the Lord Jesus would deliver him from the attacks of this messenger of Satan. In moments of physical suffering it is natural to seek relief from the One who is 'touched with the feeling of our infirmities' [*Heb* 4.15], 'and the Greek word for "besought" is one frequently used of the appeals of the sick in the Gospels' (Goudge).

*V*9: **And he hath said unto me, My grace is sufficient for thee: for *my* power is made perfect in weakness. Most gladly therefore will I rather glory in my weaknesses, that the power of Christ may rest upon me.**

And he hath said unto me, 'The perfect tense denotes that what the Lord said was a *standing* answer valid for the Apostle's whole life' (Waite).

My grace is sufficient for thee: for *my* power is made perfect in weakness. Two thoughts intertwine here: 1. You will get no more, Paul's request being denied [*v* 8], and 2. You need no more, since 'my power is made perfect in weakness' (H. Conzelmann, *TDNT*, Vol. IX, p. 395). Christ's grace is sufficient in that it does not banish weakness, but overcomes it by making it the vehicle of his royal power. None is too weak to be of service to Christ, but many are too strong to be used by him [1 *Cor* 1.27]. It is because the Lord will have all the glory that he uses those who are acutely aware of their own weakness [1 *Cor* 2.3]. Paul thus reaches the climax of the entire Epistle in this revelation of the secret of his power, a secret whose meaning was far beyond the understanding of his boastful rivals. For the self-sufficient must ever remain strangers to the power of that grace which is manifested only in conscious weakness.

Most gladly therefore will I rather glory in my weaknesses, This unexpected answer resulted in a complete reversal of Paul's attitude towards his thorn in the flesh, so that he was now prepared to welcome the weaknesses which made his dependence upon the power of Christ so complete. But it is important to distinguish between Paul's weaknesses which were *given* him [*v* 7], and 'a joyless theology of insecurity' that encouraged men to try to accumulate merit before God through sufferings which were self-inflicted (so P. E. Hughes).

that the power of Christ may rest upon me. Literally, 'may pitch its tent upon me', i.e. 'dwell in me as in a tent, as the shechinah dwelt of old in the tabernacle. To be made thus the dwelling-place of the power of Christ, where he reveals his glory, was a rational ground of rejoicing in those infirmities which were the condition of his presence and the occasion for the manifestation of his power' (Hodge).

*V*10: **Wherefore I take pleasure in weaknesses, in injuries, in necessities, in persecutions, in distresses, for Christ's sake: for when I am weak, then am I strong.**

for Christ's sake: These are the all-important words which qualify the five preceding nouns. 'Only a morbid fanatic can take pleasure in the sufferings he inflicts upon himself; only an insensitive fool can take pleasure in the sufferings that are the consequences of his folly; and only a convinced Christian can take pleasure in sufferings endured *for Christ's sake*' (Tasker).

for when I am weak, then am I strong. This paradox of grace is the principle of all effective service. Paul had early learned that the treasure of the gospel is committed to frail earthen vessels, in order to show that the power belongs to God alone [4.7–10]. This is a hard lesson for us to learn, yet it brings great encouragement with it. For though we can accomplish nothing in our own strength, mountains are moved by weak men who trust in Christ's power.

*V*11: **I am become foolish: ye compelled me; for I ought to have been commended of you: for in nothing was I behind the very chiefest apostles, though I am nothing.**

Paul admits that he has become a fool, but this foolishness was forced upon him by the disloyalty of the Corinthians. For if instead of receiving the slanders of his detractors, they had rushed to his defence, he would not have been compelled to descend to the folly of boasting in order to rescue them from the toils of false doctrine. 'It is a debt we owe to good men, to stand up in the defence of their reputation; and we are under special obligation to those we have received benefit by, especially spiritual benefit, to own them as instruments in God's hand of good to us, and to vindicate them when they are calumniated by others' (Matthew Henry).

for in nothing did I fall short of the superlative apostles, nothing though I am. (Waite) ' "Nonentity" though I am, you have had ample proof that I did not fall short of these precious "apostles" of yours!' The charge hurled at Paul is a boomerang, for he has boasted of nothing but his own 'no-thingness'. Yet this nothingness has been used as the vehicle of divine power in Corinth, whereas the self-inflated pre-tensions of these super-apostles have been productive of nothing more than the works of the flesh. 'The difference between this statement and that of 11.5, is that there he asserted a general and standing non-inferiority, whereas he here asserts a non-inferiority proved in his actual ministry among them (aorist). Hence the clause is a transition-link to the appeal to facts [12ff] with which they were acquainted' (Waite).

*V*12: **Truly the signs of an apostle were wrought among you in all patience, by signs and wonders and mighty works.**

the signs that mark a true apostle were performed among you (but you paid no attention) (Arndt-Gingrich). The miraculous element in Paul's ministry should have con-vinced the Corinthians of the reality of his apostleship. For apostolic signs were the visible authentication of an apostolic commission. 'We no longer have the apostles with us and therefore the supernatural gifts (the communication of which was an essential part of "the *signs* of an apostle" (2 *Cor* 12.12) are absent' (Arthur Pink, *The Holy Spirit,* p. 179). It is obvious that such an appeal would have been ludicrous if the Corinthians had never witnessed such signs. By his use of the passive tense, Paul shows that he was but the instrument through whom the power of God was manifested in their midst. 'In all patience' is the element *in* which these signs were wrought.

by signs and wonders and mighty works. 'He calls them *signs* because they are not merely meaningless spectacles but are designed to instruct men. He calls them *wonders* because by their novelty they should rouse and astonish, and he calls them powers or *mighty works* because they are more evidently examples of divine power than those which we discover in the ordinary course of nature' (Calvin). [cf *Acts* 2.22; 2 *Thess* 2.9; *Heb* 2.4]

*V*13: **For what is there wherein ye were made inferior to the rest of the churches, except *it be* that I myself was not a burden to you? forgive me this wrong.**

Thus the ministry the Corinthians received from Paul was in no respect inferior to that which the rest of the churches received, unless it was in regard to his refusal to accept maintenance from them. With cutting irony he asks their forgiveness for this wrong! 'In my nothingness I did not ask even a penny of support. Pardon me for the great loss which you thus suffered!' (Lenski).

*V*14: **Behold, this is the third time I am ready to come to you; and I will not be a burden to you: for I seek not yours, but you: for the children ought not to lay up for the parents, but the parents for the children.**

Paul is now ready to pay them his third visit and he will not be a burden to them this time any more than he was on his two previous visits, the first of which took place when he founded the church, and the second 'painful' visit towards the end of his stay in Ephesus [cf 2.1 and see Introduction].

for I seek not yours, but you: Paul has a far greater goal in view than a share of their wealth; he seeks their full salvation through the grace of God in Christ Jesus. He cares not for their goods so long as he can gain their souls. His concern is not for the wool, but for the sheep [cf 1 *Pet* 5.2].

children ... parents As their spiritual father [1 *Cor* 4.14, 15), Paul does not seek earthly treasure *from* them, but rather seeks to lay up heavenly treasure *for* them!

*V*15: **And I will most gladly spend and be spent for your souls. If I love you more abundantly, am I loved the less?**

Paul's more than fatherly affection for the Corinthians was proved by his willingness to spend and 'be spent out' (ASV margin) for the good of their souls. But it would be an unhappy irony if his increasing love resulted in a diminishing return from them. 'That would be a strange kind of return to make, a strange instance of inverse proportion!' (Plummer).

*V*16: **But be it so, I did not myself burden you; but, being crafty, I caught you with guile.**
That Paul himself had never been a burden on the Corinthians' resources could not be disputed by anyone, but his detractors had not been above hinting that he had profited from them in other ways. The insinuation was that 'with my natural craft, I caught you by my ostentatious disinterestedness, and then all the more successfully plundered you through my agents' (Massie).

*V*17: **Did I take advantage of you by any one of them whom I have sent unto you?** 18 **I exhorted Titus, and I**

sent the brother with him. Did Titus take any advantage of you? walked we not in the same spirit? *walked we* **not in the same steps?**

Paul throws down the challenge in the confidence that the transparent honesty of his assistants speaks for itself. Titus appears to have visited Corinth at least three times: first to start the collection [8.6a]; then as the bearer of the 'severe' letter; and finally to complete the collection [8.6b, 16–24]. As the false apostles had questioned the financial integrity of Paul's representatives [v 16], these verses must refer to the first visit of Titus, and perhaps 'the brother' who was his companion on that occasion was also chosen by Paul to help in the completion of the gracious work [8.22]. By appealing to the success of Titus in winning the Corinthians' trust, Paul would also have them know that the character and conduct of the messenger was a faithful reflection of the apostle upon whose instructions he had acted.

*V*19: **Ye think all this time that we are excusing ourselves unto you. In the sight of God speak we in Christ. But all things, beloved,** *are* **for your edifying.**

Have you been thinking all along that we have been defending ourselves to you? (NIV) Paul's self-vindication is complete but he does not want the Corinthians to run away with the idea that he stands before their tribunal in the hope of securing a favourable verdict.

We have been speaking in the sight of God as those in Christ; (NIV) It is not to *men* that Paul holds himself accountable [1 Cor 4.3], for it is in the sight of God and in union with Christ that he so speaks [cf 2.17].

and everything we do, dear friends, is for your strengthening. (NIV) 'So far as his authority in Corinth was undermined, so far were they tottering and it was necessary to reconsolidate *his* position in order that *theirs* might be restored and secured' (Waite).

*V*20: **For I fear, lest by any means, when I come, I should find you not such as I would, and should myself be found of you such as ye would not; lest by any means** *there should be* **strife, jealousy, wraths, factions, backbitings, whisperings, swellings, tumults;**

Although Paul has spoken so sternly, it has been with a view to their edification, for he fears that when he comes he may find them in a different state than *he* would wish, i.e. still wallowing in the same sins which had called forth his severe reproofs. In that case, they would find him to be other than *they* would wish, i.e. severe in punishing their misconduct. He gently gives expression to his fear in the hope that they will take the opportunity to remove all occasion for such severity before he arrives in Corinth. The list of vices seems to be arranged in four pairs: contention and envying; fits of temper and party-intrigues; open slander and secret gossip; swellings of pride and grave disorders.

*V*21: **lest again when I come my God should humble me before you, and I should mourn for many of them that have sinned heretofore, and repented not of the uncleanness and fornication and lasciviousness which they committed.**

Having once visited them in sorrow [2.1], Paul fears a further humiliation may be in store for him on his return to Corinth. 'Nothing brings a Christian teacher into the dust so much as the defection of those whom he has looked on as fruits of his

labour and as his crown of rejoicing' (Beet). He therefore
wonders whether he will find that many, having relapsed
into their old pagan ways, remained impenitent under his reproofs. His coming will discover whether he must mourn
over them as those who are spiritually dead.

CHAPTER THIRTEEN

On Paul's third visit the unrepentant shall have an unwelcome proof of his authority in the punishment he will not fail to administer [vv 1–4]. But instead of forcing him to provide them with such proofs, they will do better to prove the reality of their own faith [vv 5, 6]. He prays that they may be so restored that severity will not be necessary, even if he is thus made to appear weak. He would far sooner write severely to them than deal severely with them when present, because his power was given to build up and not to cast down [vv 7–10]. He closes the letter with a final exhortation, greetings, and his farewell prayer for them all [vv 11–14].

*V*1: **This is the third time I am coming to you. At the mouth of two witnesses or three shall every word be established.**

Paul abruptly announces the imminence of this *third* visit, That he *is* coming is certain, but the manner of his visit will depend upon the Corinthians' attitude towards him. He wishes no one to be in the slightest doubt of his determination to deal with the recalcitrant in accordance with the principles of justice laid down by Moses and endorsed by Christ [*Deut* 19.15; *Matt* 18.16]. 'Paul's word is intended as a warning. He has just mentioned repentance [12.21]. He hopes that there will be no unrepentant sinners with whom he must deal when he arrives. They will get a fair trial, indeed, but a trial they will get' (Lenski).

*V*2: **I have said beforehand, and I do say beforehand, as when I was present the second time, so now, being absent, to them that have sinned heretofore, and to all the rest, that, if I come again, I will not spare;**

As Bengel notes, there is in the text, 'an uninterrupted chiasmus throughout the three members of the sentence', which P. E. Hughes sets out as follows:—

I have said beforehand	and	I do say beforehand
↓		↓
when I was present the second time	and	now being absent
↓		↓
to them that have sinned heretofore	and	to all the rest

Paul has already warned those who were leading sinful lives at the time of his second visit that if he came again he would not spare them, and now he reiterates the warning to all others whom he may find in the same sinful state when he arrives in Corinth for the third time.

if I come again, The meaning is: 'when I come this time' (NEB). It would be ridiculous to take the 'if' as expressed uncertainty over the much-advertised visit. 'All that is meant is that the punishment depends on the coming, whenever that takes place' (Massie).

I will not spare; Paul hopes that it will not be necessary to provide the Corinthians with the proof that he means what he says [*vv* 7, 10], but those who disregard this final warning must realize that they leave their apostle with no alternative [*v* 3].

*V*3: **seeing that ye seek a proof of Christ that speaketh in me; who to you-ward is not weak, but is powerful in you:**

This is closely connected with the previous verse ('I will not spare; seeing that . . .'). Since the Corinthians demand a proof that Christ speaks in Paul, they shall have what they want! It is possible that there is an implied contrast with his opponents' claim to be the true spokesmen of Christ. Thus Waite comments: 'The words *in me* are obviously emphatic, and show that the Christ who spoke *in him* is contrasted with the Christ which spoke in the Judaizers. In accordance with their entire system, they ascribed the weakness shown on his second visit to the Christ whom he preached and who, being not a legal, but a spiritual Christ, they said was powerless to enforce obedience to law. Thus they challenged his Christ to a proof of his power. The libertines by their defiance did the same thing, for if they did not take up the taunt of the Judaizers, they clearly counted upon the same weakness for escaping punishment altogether'.

who to you-ward is not weak, but is powerful in you: 'Of Christ's power *towards* and *among* the Corinthians, Paul has already given full proof, viz. [12.12] the miracles wrought in their midst and [3.2] the spiritual effects of the Gospel in their hearts. He will now add the more terrible proof of special punishment' (Beet).

*V*4: **for he was crucified through weakness, yet he liveth through the power of God. For we also are weak in him, but we shall live with him through the power of God toward you.**

As it was in virtue of his self-assumed weakness that Christ was once crucified, so it is in virtue of the power of God that he now lives for ever as the triumphant Son of Man. It would be folly to presume on a temporary weakness, and to forget the present reality of Christ's power to punish as well as to save. For 'the cross does *not* exhaust Christ's relation to sin; he passed from the cross to the throne, and when he comes again it is as Judge' (Denney).

If Paul has experienced in full measure what it means to be weak in Christ, he is no stranger to that divine power which is made perfect in weakness. Thus though his 'painful' visit was marked by a weakness which the Corinthians despised, when he comes again he will act towards them with a power which will command their respect! Thus the believer's future inheritance is not in view here.

V5: **Try your own selves, whether ye are in the faith; prove your own selves. Or know ye not as to your own selves, that Jesus Christ is in you? unless indeed ye be reprobate. 6 But I hope that ye shall know that we are not reprobate.**

Instead of putting Paul's apostleship to the proof [*v* 3], the Corinthians should be testing the genuineness of their own faith in Christ! If, as Paul expects, most of them find that this self-examination confirms the reality of their attachment to Christ, then it must also show that he has exercised an authentic ministry among them [3.2; 1 *Cor* 9.2]. In this passage 're-probate' is not used in the theological sense of being judicially abandoned to everlasting perdition; it means 'failing to pass the test, unapproved, counterfeit' (Souter). 'They ought to recognize Christ as a power in themselves – unless indeed they, being counterfeit Christians, cannot recognize him because he is not there' (Massie). But should any among them prove to be such counterfeit Christians, Paul hopes to convince them that at least *he* is not a counterfeit apostle! For faithfulness to his commission will compel him to mete out condign punishment to the faithless in Corinth.

*V*7: **Now we pray to God that ye do no evil; not that we may appear approved, but that ye may do that which is honourable, though we be as reprobate.**

Paul, however, prays that the Corinthians may do that which is noble and right, for he has no desire to demonstrate his apostolic authority by inflicting punishment. His first concern is not with his own reputation, but with the spiritual well-being of his converts. Hence if none deserved punishment he would not be disappointed, even though in failing to carry out a threatened judgment he might *seem like* a counterfeit apostle!

*V*8: **For we can do nothing against the truth, but for the truth.**

For, as Paul explains, he has no power to act against the truth, but only for the truth. Should he come to Corinth and find that their conduct was in conformity with the truth of the gospel, there would be no occasion to demonstrate his power in punishing the disobedient. But he would be opposing the truth, if he preferred them to do wrong because it gave him the opportunity of proving his power.

*V*9: **For we rejoice, when we are weak, and ye are strong: this we also pray for, even your perfecting.**

The apostle has no desire to appear strong among them, but is glad to be weak when their strength in well-doing requires no punishment or censure. In fact, the burden of his prayer for them is that they might be restored to spiritual wholeness. The word used here denotes 'a resetting of what has been broken and dislocated, and hence a restoration of harmonious and efficient functioning. It carries no suggestion of what is known theologically as "perfectionism" ' (P. E. Hughes).

*V*10: **For this cause I write these things while absent, that I may not when present deal sharply, according to the authority which the Lord gave me for building up, and not for casting down.**

'He would not write to them severely from a distance [10.10] except for the purpose of avoiding severity of action when present. With all his resolve to punish, with all the authority which the Lord gave him to punish, he will do anything rather than punish. This he expresses by repeating what he said in 10.8, that the true end for which his authority was given was to build up and not to pull down. However necessary or beneficial chastisement may be, it is still "a pulling down", because it is, in the form here contemplated by him, plucking out stones, for a season at least, from the temple of the Lord. It is that evil which he prays they may not bring about [*v* 7]' (Waite).

*V*11: **Finally, brethren, farewell. Be perfected: be comforted; be of the same mind; live in peace: and the God of love and peace shall be with you.**

Mend your ways, heed my appeal, (RSV) The apostle's farewell exhortation sums up his message to the Corinthians. Their many deficiencies must be amended, for the wholeness (or holiness) of the body to which they belong depends upon the harmonious working together of its many members (cf the meaning of 'perfecting' in *v* 9). But if this desirable end is to be attained in Corinth, they must so heed his appeal as to act upon it.

be of the same mind; live in peace: They must seek to be 'of the same mind in the Lord' [*Phil* 4.2], for they can only live in peace when they set their minds on the same thing. To have the mind of Christ is to banish that selfish way of thinking which always fosters strife.

and the God of love and peace shall be with you. 'We have here the familiar Christian paradox. God's presence produces love and peace, and we must have love and peace in order to have his presence. God gives what he commands. God gives, but we must cherish his gifts. His agency does not supersede ours, but mingles with it and becomes one with it in our consciousness. We work out our own salvation, while God works in us' (Hodge). [*Phil* 2.12, 13] Thus the believer becomes actively engaged in doing the will of God through the enabling power of the same Spirit by whom he was first quickened.

*V*12: **Salute one another with a holy kiss. 13 All the saints salute you.**

The kiss of peace was the customary greeting among friends in the East, and its early adoption by believers invested it with a deeper meaning. It was a holy kiss because it expressed the communion they enjoyed through their sharing together in the peace of God, and was exchanged before the Lord's Supper as a sign of mutual forgiveness. [cf *Rom* 16.16; 1 *Cor* 16.20]. But later abuses brought the practice into disrepute, and it was eventually abandoned by the Western church. 'It is not a command of perpetual obligation, as the spirit of the command is that Christians should express their mutual love in the way sanctioned by the age and community in which they live' (Hodge). As an expression of the church's unity, Paul follows his usual practice of sending the greetings of the 'saints' [cf 1 *Cor* 1.2] with whom he is in touch when despatching the letter, i.e. the Christians of Macedonia.

*V*14: **The grace of the Lord Jesus Christ, and the love of God, and the communion of the Holy Spirit, be with you all.**

'Remarkable it is that an Epistle written under a tempest of conflicting emotions, breathing in some places indignation, reproach, and sadness, at being driven to self-vindication against worthless detractors who should never have been listened to – that precisely this Epistle is the one that closes with the richest and most comprehensive of all the benedictions in the New Testament, the one which the Christian church in every land and of every age has found, and will find as long as the world lasts, the most available for public use, as a close to its worship' (Brown)

The grace of the Lord Jesus Christ, The Pauline gospel is summed up in the word which is his distinctive signature in every epistle. He who was once the implacable enemy of gospel grace is now its doughtiest defender. As the unworthy recipient of God's grace, he is inexorably opposed to the self-sufficient moralism by which it is subverted, always insistent that it comes to helpless sinners as the unmerited favour of God in Christ. It cannot be bought; it cannot be earned; it must be received as a free gift. Hence the order here is the order of Christian experience, for it is only through the grace of the Lord Jesus Christ that sinners come to know the love of God for them. The full title sets forth the majesty of the Mediator. 'Lord' points to his essential Deity, 'Jesus' underlines his genuine humanity so willingly assumed for our salvation, while 'Christ' tells us that he is the Messiah, the anointed fulfiller of the promised redemption.

and the love of God, Although God loved his people with an everlasting love, his holiness could not overlook the reality of their fearful fall into sin. In the resolution of this dilemma at the cross, the divine wisdom comes to its sublimest expression. It is there that all the attributes of God are seen to harmonize in the dread judgment that vindicated his justice even as it published his mercy. Thus the eternal love of God was the secret source of that matchless grace through which there is now manifested the marvel of the Father's adopting love.

and the communion of the Holy Spirit, Apart from the cross there can be no real understanding of God's love, while the only lasting fellowship between men is the fellowship of sinners redeemed by Christ's blood. It is the work of the Holy Spirit to bring about this fellowship by applying the benefits of that redemption to the hearts of God's people. It is therefore upon his gracious work that the individual and corporate spiritual life of believers entirely depends.

be with you all. Here is the measure of Paul's magnanimity; his love embraces *all* the Corinthians, even those who have been the most disaffected towards him.

'The distinct personality and divinity of the Son, the Father, and the Holy Spirit, to each of whom prayer is addressed, is here taken for granted. And therefore this passage is a clear recognition of the doctrine of the Trinity, which is the fundamental doctrine of Christianity. For a Christian is one who seeks and enjoys the grace of the Lord Jesus, the love of God, and the communion of the Holy Ghost' (Hodge).

Soli Deo Gloria

BIBLIOGRAPHY

Arndt, W. F.–Gingrich, F. W., *A Greek-English Lexicon of the New Testament* (University of Chicago Press, 1957)

Barrett, C. K., *The Second Epistle to the Corinthians* (BNTC) (A & C Black, 1973)

Beet, J. A., *II Corinthians* (Hodder & Stoughton, 1882)

Bengel, J. A., *Gnomon of the New Testament* Vol. III (T & T Clark, 1857)

Bernard, J. H., *II Corinthians* (EGT) (Eerdmans, 1974)

Boettner, Loraine, *The Reformed Doctrine of Predestination* (Presbyterian & Reformed, 1965)

Brown, David, *II Corinthians* (Popular Commentary on the NT) (T & T Clark, 1882)

Bruce, F. F., *An Expanded Paraphrase of the Epistles of Paul* (Paternoster, 1965)

Bruce, F. F., *1 and 2 Corinthians* (NCB) (Oliphants, 1971)

Bruce, F. F., *Paul: Apostle of the Free Spirit* (Paternoster, 1977)

Bruce, F. F., *The Acts of the Apostles* (NICNT) (Marshall, Morgan and Scott, 1956)

Bruner, Frederick Dale, *A Theology of the Holy Spirit* (Hodder & Stoughton, 1971)

Calvin, John, *II Corinthians – Philemon* (St. Andrews Press, 1964)

Chantry, Walter J., *Signs of the Apostles* (Banner of Truth, 1976)

Denney, James, *II Corinthians* (EB) (Hodder & Stoughton, 1894)

Denney, James, *The Death of Christ* (Tyndale, 1964)

Dickson, David, *The Psalms* (Banner of Truth, 1959)

Douglas, J. D. (Editor), *The New Bible Dictionary* (IVP, 1962)

Fairbairn, Patrick, *The Interpretation of Prophecy* (Banner of Truth, 1964)

BIBLIOGRAPHY

Fausset, A. R., *II Corinthians* (JFB) (Collins, 1874)

Filson, Floyd V., *The Second Epistle to the Corinthians* (IB) (Abingdon, 1953)

Geldenhuys, Norval, *Supreme Authority* (Marshall, Morgan & Scott, 1953)

Goudge, H. L., *II Corinthians* (WC) (Methuen, 1927)

Guthrie, Donald, *New Testament Introduction* (Tyndale, 1970)

Harris, Murray J., *2 Corinthians* (EBC) (Zondervan, 1976)

Henry, Matthew, *Commentary on the Holy Bible* (various editions)

Hodge, A. A., *The Confession of Faith* (Banner of Truth, 1958)

Hodge, Charles, *II Corinthians* (Banner of Truth, 1959)

Hughes, Philip E., *II Corinthians* (NICNT) (Marshall, Morgan & Scott, 1961)

Jenkyn, William, *Exposition of the Epistle of Jude* (James & Klock, 1976)

Kittel, G. – Friedrich, G., *Theological Dictionary of the New Testament* Vols. 1–10 (Eerdmans, 1964–1976) (translated by Geoffrey W. Bromiley: index by Ronald E. Pitkin)

Lenski, R. C. H., *The Interpretation of I & II Corinthians* (Augsburg, 1961)

Lightfoot, J. B., *Notes on the Epistles of St. Paul* (Zondervan, 1957)

Machen, J. G., *The Origin of Paul's Religion* (Eerdmans, 1925)

Martin, R. P. (contributor), *Daily Bible Commentary 4* (Scripture Union, 1974)

Martin, R. P. (contributor), *New Testament Foundations – 2* (Paternoster, 1978)

Massie, J., *I & II Corinthians* (CB) (Caxton, n.d.)

Meeter, John E. (Editor), *The Shorter Writings of B. B. Warfield* Vol. I (Presbyterian & Reformed, 1970)

Menzies, Allan, *II Corinthians* (Macmillan, 1912)

Murray, John, *Redemption – Accomplished and Applied* (Banner of Truth, 1961)

Murray, John, *Collected Writings: 1* (Banner of Truth, 1976)

Murray, John, *Collected Writings: 2* (Banner of Truth, 1977)

Pink, Arthur W., *Gleanings from Paul* (Moody, 1967)

Plummer, Alfred, *II Corinthians* (ICC) (T & T Clark, 1915)

Poole, Matthew, *A Commentary on the Holy Bible* Vol. III (Banner of Truth, 1963)

Ridderbos, Herman, *Paul and Jesus* (Presbyterian & Reformed, 1957)

Robinson, J. Armitage, *St. Paul's Epistle to the Ephesians* (James Clarke, n.d.)

Smeaton, George, *The Apostles' Doctrine of the Atonement* (Zondervan, 1957)

Souter, A., *A Pocket Lexicon to the Greek New Testament* (Oxford, 1956)

Tasker, R. V. G., *II Corinthians* (TNTC) (Tyndale, 1958)

Tasker, R. V. G., *The Old Testament in the New Testament* (SCM, 1946)

Trapp, John, *Commentary on the New Testament* (Sovereign Grace, 1958)

Trench, R. C., *Synonyms of the New Testament* (James Clarke, 1961)

Vincent, Marvin, R., *Word Studies in the New Testament* (Macdonald, n.d.)

Vine, W. E., *Expository Dictionary of New Testament Words* (Oliphants, 1958)

Vos, Geerhardus, *Biblical Theology* (Banner of Truth, 1975)

Vos, Geerhardus, *Pauline Eschatology* (Eerdmans, 1961)

Wand, J. W. C., *A History of the Early Church* (Methuen, 1937)

Waite, Joseph, *II Corinthians* (Speaker's Commentary) (John Murray, 1881)